T0209309

LIONHEARTED LEADERSHIP

MINISTERING FOR THE LONG HAUL

RICHARD H. ADDISON JR.

WESTBOW
PRESS®
A DIVISION OF THOMAS NELSON
& ZONDERVAN

WestBow Press books may be ordered through booksellers or by contacting:

WestBow Press
A Division of Thomas Nelson & Zondervan
1663 Liberty Drive
Bloomington, IN 47403
www.westbowpress.com
844-714-3454

ISBN: 979-8-3850-0287-0 (sc)
ISBN: 979-8-3850-0406-5 (hc)
ISBN: 979-8-3850-0286-3 (e)

Library of Congress Control Number: 2023913042

Print information available on the last page.

WestBow Press rev. date: 07/27/2023

Endorsements

"Some leaders are born. Some leaders are made. Rick Addison was both. I believe he was born to be a natural leader and the circumstances of his life forged those skills with fire. I had the privilege of his friendship and mentorship for 29 years and it was an incalculable inspiration in my life and career."

- Sam Mullinax
  CEO Lenco Marine Inc.

"Pastor Rick was the hardest working pastor I have ever met. He lived Paul's words to be steadfast, unmovable, always abounding in the work of the Lord. Pastor Rick was my friend and we met for 15 years one time a month to share our hearts with each other."

- Dan Plourde- Pastor has been in ministry for 28 years. He has been Pastor of Calvary Chapel, Jupiter, Florida 25 years ago. He has BA in Social Science with an emphasis in Social Services. A MS in Counseling Psychology and completed the coursework towards an MA Religion

"Rick Addison was not only a great friend, but he was also a great pastor and leader as well. I enjoyed our conversations together on a regular basis. He always amazed me with his wisdom and vision for the future. He had great wisdom in business matters and in everyday life concerns."

- Allen Milam- co founder of Milam's Markets serving Miami, Florida since 1984 with six supermarkets.

"Rick's principles of leadership as my pastor and friend influenced my personal life as well as my 30 year career in the fire service. His life always exemplified integrity, loyalty, vision, and steadfastness."

- David Cantrell, Battalion Chief, Stuart Fire Rescue (Ret), Stuart, Florida

"My friend Rick Addison was a lion hearted leader for sure! His strategic energy, intentional focus, ministry successes all testify to his generous investment in people. He lived out what he believed! I have been blessed to witness and learn from the exceptional leadership skills of my friend of 25 years Rick Addison.

- Rev. Chris Cravens has served as a lead pastor for 25 years. He is Conference President of the Heartland Regional Conference of the Bible Methodist Connection of Churches since 2017 in Ohio. He serves on multiple non-profit organizational leadership boards. He is Law Enforcement Chaplain for all departments in north Ohio area.

"I had the privilege of meeting Pastor Rick in 2014, when he came for the first time to Spain to be part of a leadership training process. We walked along with him in this challenge for 3 years. Pastor Rick became our friend and mentor. He believed and took a chance on my wife Ani and me at a time when we were just starting to look after our church in Valencia, Spain. At that moment, we were only a congregation of 35 people, but with a lot of passion and the dream to build what God was calling us to do. Pastor Rick not only has been an inspiration, and a reason to challenge ourselves, but he was also a father to us who not only invested his wisdom, time, and love, but also his resources into our lives and church. His legacy lives on here, in this country and in every place where God allows us to bless. That is why I am sure that every page of this book you are reading about church and leadership will be a great blessing to your life and ministry. It will challenge you to believe in a God of the impossible and will lead you to see that every principle you put into practice will produce great results. Open your heart, raise your expectations, and let God speak to you through the life of a hero of faith like Pastor Rick."

- ◦ Nestor Salas, Pastor of Centro Cristiano Esperanza Valencia, Spain

CONTENTS

PREFACE

My father, known widely as Pastor Rick, was the most amazing man I have ever known. When I was younger, I didn't appreciate his level of integrity and character that has now become a legacy for me and my kids. For the past twenty or so years, my father dealt with congenital heart failure, which affected his health, especially in the final year of his life. He passed away in June 2022 and left behind a legacy that few could ever imagine. Per his request, his tombstone reads, "He served his generation, and then he died." The lessons of leadership and personal integrity that I learned from him are a treasure worth more than wealth.

One of the best memories of my dad was when I went deer hunting with him in Alabama. He would always say, "Eric, always leave the woods better than you found it." He lived this mantra not only while hunting but also in every aspect of his life. He was committed to leaving his relationships, his possessions, and his family better than he found them.

We are all better for knowing him, and I know that as you read this book you will find timeless truths that will help you in your ministry or as you lead your organization.

INTRODUCTION

The LORD your God is with you, the Mighty Warrior who saves. He will take great delight in you; in his love he will no longer rebuke you, but will rejoice over you with singing. (Zephaniah 3:17 NIV)

I love the church of Jesus Christ. There is nothing more exciting, more rewarding, more inspiring to me than the body of Christ thriving in a local community. There is nothing like seeing the transforming power of the gospel of Jesus Christ working in peoples' lives. On the other hand, I do not believe there is anything more heartbreaking than a church in the process of dying a slow death. I have seen churches that are one hundred fifty years old experiencing the dynamic work of God in their congregations. But these churches are not undergoing such vitality because they carry on like always. The *dynamic* work of God is also a *fresh* work of God.

I am writing this book because I have sensed a growing need for a resource such as this for church leaders. Having served five churches in four states over the past forty-two years of pastoral ministry, I have a rather good understanding of the unique needs of pastors and church leaders. Although the first four churches I pastored grew (by their standards, somewhat dramatically), none of them had over 150 people in attendance.

As a pastor, I would find myself looking at my efforts, and at my churches, wondering, *"There has to be a key that will unlock the doors of exponential growth."* Although I was reading everything I could find on leadership and church growth and attending seminars on this subject, it seemed I could not find a way to bring the different pieces together as a whole. In June 1993 while I continued searching and studying, God called on me to serve as the pastor of what was then called Community Bible Chapel, now The Grace Place Church, in Stuart, Florida.

When my wife, Karon, and I came to the church, it was approximately sixteen years old, and I was its third pastor. The founding pastor had served the church for twelve years, and the second pastor served for four. When we arrived, the church averaged around 125 for morning worship attendance. The church experienced a real surge of growth during its early years, with attendance peaking briefly at nearly three hundred.

But the church then settled into a repetitive pattern of growing to nearly two hundred, then declining to about one hundred. The reasons for the up-and-down process were never analyzed or dealt with. Because of this and a variety of other reasons, many people in the congregation were frustrated over a lack of focus and direction.

God had been stretching and developing me during those first fourteen years I was serving the four previous churches. In His incredible providence, God was able to help us bring the pieces together, and He began doing something through the ministry development of The Grace Place Church that neither I nor the church had ever experienced.

The church transitioned from a very introverted church, focused on itself and survival, to an outreach-focused church willing to do whatever necessary to reach the community with the hope of the gospel of Jesus Christ. We moved from a traditional to a contemporary style of worship, and we grew from those few hundred people to over fifteen hundred in attendance. As I tell people all the time, "We have only just begun."

I realize so many churches could be described the way ours was when I found it in 1993. I have talked to pastors and leaders in many other churches who tell me they have tried everything, but nothing has worked in a sustained way. Trying one more gimmick is not going to solve a leadership problem, a spiritual problem, a problem within the organizational structures of the church, a philosophical problem, or the problem of having either no strategies or the wrong strategies.

But this material is not a bunch of new techniques for you or your church to imitate—it is based upon principles that are applicable in churches of all types and in many different places. What we have learned will work in the Midwest as well as it does in South Florida. It will work in the Southwest as well as in the Northeast.

In this book, I address several key areas needed for the church to advance the kingdom of Christ. When these components come together, the church benefits in amazing ways. If I knew forty-two years ago what I am sharing with you in this book now, I believe any of the four churches I pastored could have experienced similar dynamics to those of The Grace Place.   For example, a church can have a pastor who is a tremendous leader and a real man of God, but if he is dealing with church structures that tie his leadership hands behind his back, then the only development the church will experience is related to what the pastor can do relationally. When he becomes discouraged and leaves the church (and he will!), most of the growth the church experienced leaves with him. Or, put the other way, if a church has great organizational structures and the right philosophy, but has a weak or spiritually shallow leader, the church will never realize its potential. If a church has a great, godly leader along with good church structures and philosophy but does not have a strategy to reach the community and world with the hope of the gospel of Christ, then the church will only experience part of what God wants to do. The key to a church experiencing sustained development is to have all three elements working together to accomplish God's purposes for His church.

After years of analyzing churches and congregations, it has become evident that when any of these key components are missing, the church will either gradually decline, become static, or go through the up-and-down syndrome The Grace Place went through during the years preceding my arrival.

What I am going to share with you in this book is the material that you can probably find in only a few other resources. I believe that, just as God helped us do with The Grace Place, He can use this book to do the same thing in your ministry and church.

Let me challenge you to let God use this book to "connect the dots" so that your church can become all that God wants it to be! I know God wants to do something truly powerful through your ministry to advance His kingdom through your church. As I have been writing this book, my constant prayer has been that God will use this book for precisely that purpose.

CHAPTER 1

The Long Haul

Pastors who serve for the "long haul" and are considered lionhearted leaders have one consistent characteristic that always jumps out—they are passionate about what they do. They are passionate about their relationship with God, about their ministry, about reaching irreligious people with the gospel, about their goals and strategies, and about their churches. There is a fire burning in their souls to do something for God that makes an everlasting difference in the lives of the people within the sphere of their ministry influence.

The Bible is filled with stories of superachievers—men like Nehemiah, who rebuilt the walls of Jerusalem in just fifty-two days, or the apostle Paul, who said, "I do not consider myself yet to have taken hold of it. But one thing I do: Forgetting what is behind and straining toward what is ahead, I press on toward the goal to win the prize for which God has called me heavenward in Christ Jesus" (Philippians 3:13–14 NIV). The common characteristic in their lives is a passion to accomplish their God-assigned task.

Over the years as I have worked with staff members and pastors, I have discovered that I can teach them leadership skills and how to strategize, but I cannot teach them to be passionate about ministry. Passion comes from knowing *this is what I was created to do.* The Bible states that while you were "being knit together in your mother's womb," God was formulating an incredible plan for your life. Your chromosomes were arranged the way they are, and your personality was shaped the way it is, so you could accomplish God's purpose for your life. How can you help but be passionate about ministry if it is what you are called by God to do?

Counting the Costs

If you are going to lead a church for the long haul, now is the time to count the costs. Serving for the long haul will cost you energy, time, money, and sleep. There will be people who love you and people who hate you; some people will think you are a hero, and others will think you are a zero. It is easy to look at big buildings, beautiful campuses, large staffs, and perks and privileges and not see the blood, sweat, and tears. Jesus makes it clear that there is a tremendous cost in following Him. He makes it equally clear that if we are going to follow Him, we need to count the cost before we begin ministry. This is how He puts it in Luke 9:57–62 (NIV):

> As they were walking along the road, a man said to him, "I will follow you wherever you go." Jesus replied, "Foxes have holes and birds of the air have nests, but the Son of Man has no place to lay his head." He said to another man, "Follow me." But the man replied, "Lord, first let me go and bury my father." Jesus said to him, "Let the dead bury their own dead, but you go and proclaim the kingdom of God." Still another said, "I will follow you, Lord; but first let me go back and say good-bye to my family." Jesus replied, "No one who

puts his hand to the plow and looks back is fit for service in the kingdom of God."

I have had pastors of other churches tell me, "Rick, I wouldn't do what you do for anything in the world." Many pastors start well, but they do not have the devotion, commitment, and perseverance, or what I call the "stick-to-it-ness," to see their ministry through challenging times. They see the time and challenges I deal with daily, and they say things like, "I am not willing to pay the price to see that through." When I hear that, I am reminded that it is imperative to count the costs before you begin.

This Is What I Was Born to Do

The determination to stay on the job comes when a pastor knows *this is what I was created to do.* When pastors bail out of ministry in the tough times, it always causes tremendous confusion for both believers and unbelievers.

Years ago, I had a series of conversations with a very gifted man who had worked in the business world and now believed God had called him into church ministry. During several meetings with him and his wife, we discussed what Jesus says about making these decisions carelessly and casually. They both assured me that they had prayed about it and agreed this was what God wanted them to do with their lives.

Eventually, we hired him to serve on our staff as an assistant pastor in charge of small groups. It did not take long for me to discover that his primary passion was making money, and his second passion was to take the maximum amount of time off. He was not willing to be flexible with the needs of people. He began to complain about his job requirements, which caused confusion both inside and outside the church. Within fourteen months, he and his wife both reevaluated and decided that he wasn't "called" to do church ministry after all.

It is imperative to count the costs and to know what the commitment to serving as a pastor is before you put your hand to the plow.

Understanding the call of God in my life began when I was a senior in high school. It was then that I came to a personal faith in Jesus. It did not take long for me to have a growing awareness that God's plan for my life was to serve Him as a pastor. This was a huge challenge for various reasons.

First, my dad was a pastor of a smaller church until his untimely death in an automobile accident when I was fourteen years old. I knew my dad was never going to get rich on the salary he was making. When God began talking to me about serving Him as a pastor, the money thing became a big challenge. I learned the drywall trade in my midteens, and by the time I was sixteen years old, I was subcontracting and running my own crew. I was making good money as a high school student and realized I had a knack for business. I knew I could create my own company and make a lot of money. A call to vocational ministry felt like I was taking a vow of poverty!

Second, I knew that submitting to God's plan for my life was going to require years of schooling and training. It would involve studying things like Greek and theology, subjects that had always seemed rather boring to me.

Third, it was a battle of will. I had plans for my life laid out that involved business and making money. God knew all that, and He persisted in making it clear to me that serving Him as a pastor was exactly what He wanted me to do, regardless of the costs.

CHAPTER 2

Passion and Purpose

I can remember as if it were yesterday, sitting in a church service and wrestling with a call to ministry. I was only seventeen years old, and I wanted to make sure that this call was not just based on the emotions of the moment. As I felt the pull of the Holy Spirit, my mind raced as I nervously got up from my seat and made my way to the altar to answer the call.

That response was immediately affirmed by many people in our church and by family members. From that day to the present, I have lived with an acute awareness that serving God as a pastor was what I was born to do. During the best of times and the worst of times, that sense of purpose has never wavered in my life.

Frequently, people come to me wanting to know whether God is "calling" them to serve in ministry. My response is always the same—"If you are called to do this, you will never be able to find contentment doing anything else."

Our first church was challenging, which is a real understatement. When I resigned from that church, as my wife and I were working through the aftermath of that experience, she asked me a question.

"Rick, after all we have been through here, don't you think it would be helpful to take a year off?"

I looked at her and said, "Karon, you know how heartbreaking this experience has been. But I cannot think of anything more miserable than to take a year off to do something else. I know this is what God called me to do, and I know He will bless us in His time with a positive response to our ministry."

Over the years, I have had many company leaders tell me that if I were in the business arena, I would excel. I am sure that I could do well in that area, but I would never find contentment or fulfillment doing anything other than what God has called and equipped me to do—serving Him as a pastor.

Often, people in the church will express their concern that I could burn myself out. They are well-meaning, but they come from a different perspective on "career" versus "calling." Their work experiences have usually been within an environment where they have a "job," and they do not understand the difference between that and when a pastor has a "calling." When you are convinced *this is what I was born to do*, it transforms your vocation into a passion and focus on doing what God created you to do. I have said many times that if I could afford to, I would do what I do as a pastor for no financial compensation because this is what I love and what I was born to do.

Marry Well

> Find a good spouse, you find a good life—and even more: the favor of GOD! (Proverbs 18:2 The Message, paraphrased)

I was seventeen years old when I said yes to God's call to serve him as a pastor. Fortunately, I had been around the church and enough pastors growing up to know that if I was going to do ministry for the long haul,

I had to marry the right kind of wife. Even at an early age, I was aware of how important that was.

I did not date a lot of girls for a variety of reasons—one being I tried to get to know the girl reasonably well before I would consider dating her. I was seeking certain character qualities, attitudes, and goals in the "right" girl.

When I met my wife, Karon, I knew there was something different about her and felt like she might be someone I would consider marrying. Shortly after we began attending the same college, we started dating.

On our second date, I told her I really enjoyed our time together and really liked her. I also shared with her God's call to service Him as a pastor and that I was committed to fulfilling that call.

"I'm not asking you to marry me, of course, but … if your future husband, whether it's me or someone else, had a calling to serve as a pastor, would you be supportive, resistant, or passive about your support of that call?"

She agreed she would pray about it. When we had our next date, I asked her where she stood regarding her support of that call.

"If my future husband was you or someone else and if being a pastor is what God wants him to do with his life, I would be very supportive," she said with a smile and a twinkle in her eyes.

We continued dating and got married in 1974. Karon has lived up to that commitment in amazing ways for over four decades now. No one has been more supportive of my call to serve God than she has been. I am eternally grateful for all the ways she has served as a ministry partner for all these years!

Passion Enables You to Lead with Confidence

If you are passionate about ministry, you will be able to lead with confidence. Timid leadership is frequently associated with a sense of insecurity a pastor has over what he believes he ought to be doing with his life. Leading a church requires taking your ministry seriously and leading with the assurance of a general going into battle, which is what we are really doing. Pastors are in an eternal battle with Satan himself! This battle is not over the control of a certain part of the earth. This battle is for the hearts and souls of people that desperately need the hope found in the gospel of Jesus Christ.

There has never been a time such as the present when the church has needed pastors to have the courage and conviction to launch an all-out attack on Satan's strongholds in their communities. You will never lead with confidence if you are ready to throw in the towel every time you run into a little difficulty.

Apostle James says, "a double-minded man, is unstable in all he does" (James 1:8 NIV). If you are constantly wavering between devotion to ministry and a desire to get out of ministry, your indecision will result in timid leadership. God calls you to serve him with *"all of your heart."* This means He wants you to serve him with total devotion and abandonment for the advancement of His kingdom.

If I were serving on the board of a business, I would not want the CEO to be constantly wavering between whether they wanted to lead the company or do something else. We understand that this kind of indecision would have a disastrous impact on a company. As the "CEO" of your church, God calls you to be single-minded in your focus of advancing His kingdom. In fact, Jesus tells us we must be found faithful in our service. Without a sense of single-mindedness to ministry, you will be ineffective in your leadership and your church will never flourish.

Satan knows this, and that is why he works so vigorously to discourage and distract us from our dedication and devotion to advancing the kingdom of God.

Lord, Deliver Me from Me

Frequently, the struggle with passion in our lives is really a spiritual battle. One of the struggles I had for many years was over what I call "pleasing men vs. pleasing God." This is a challenge that affects all pastors, but I believe the structures of many smaller churches contribute to this problem.

For example, I grew up in a church where one of the measurements of a pastor's success or failure was determined by how happy the people in the congregation were with him.

The first two churches I served had a "pastoral recall" system. Each year, the congregation would take a vote as to whether they wanted the pastor to continue his service to that church. If you made enough people unhappy, then you were going to be finding the nearest exit. This is a very unhealthy system and is characteristic of many smaller churches. In the past, Satan used that system to develop a "pleasing men" approach to my leadership. This robbed me of my passion and contributed to a fearful approach to leadership. This was a very conservative church that had rules such as what women could wear and not wear before becoming involved to minister. That timidity put a lid on my ability to lead any of those churches to grow beyond 150 in attendance.

God used a series of challenging events, a lot of frustration, and a time of spiritual renewal before I began to minister out of what I call "the fear of the Lord." We had people who could serve in the church but did not measure up to the man-made rules. So that led me to understand that I need to be primarily concerned with hearing God say, "Well done, good and faithful servant! You have been faithful with a few things; I will put you in charge of many things. Come and share your master's happiness!" (Matthew 25:21 NIV) and not live for man's approval.

I do not believe I can adequately describe the impact serving out of the "fear of the Lord" brings into your leadership. I believe it is doubtful you will ever be able to lead your church to the next level until you begin to minister this way. Unfortunately, many smaller churches are in the state they are in because their pastors are more concerned about what people think and say about them rather than what God thinks and says about them.

In the year prior to coming to serve at The Grace Place, God took me through a time of spiritual renewal. This renewal time transformed my leadership as a pastor. I was serving as the pastor of a denominational church in Birmingham, Alabama, and I had allowed myself to get distracted by what I now call the "ecclesiastical apparatus" of that denomination. Key leaders in that denomination would say to me, "You know, Rick, you're the kind of guy that we like to promote into denominational officials. You have a really bright future in this denomination." Unfortunately, I let that stuff affect my focus.

I had left a nondenominational church in Montgomery, Alabama, to go to the church in Birmingham. Looking back, the only reason I can identify that I had for going there was to pursue opportunities for denominational positions. For the very first time in my entire ministry, I experienced a church that for two years flatlined. No matter what I did or how hard I worked, nothing happened. I had never served as pastor of a church that had not grown larger with the passage of time. In my previous ministries, I could look back and see how churches developed and people were saved, but now nothing seemed to be happening.

During the summer of 1992, my family and I were in Wyoming on vacation at Yellowstone National Park. We were staying outside of Yellowstone in a little cabin. The first morning we were there, I woke up early and full of frustration about the ministry situation we were in. I got up and walked down to a mountain stream and sat on a rotting stump. For about thirty minutes I told God how mad I was about the whole thing. God, who doesn't talk to me in audible words, began to speak to my spirit.

After I had expended my anger, God began to show me some things about myself that I had completely covered up and, until that day, had never seen. He showed me that I had a problem with pride.

I thought that wherever I went, there would be "happy days" for the church. Somehow, I had allowed myself to think that I carried all the answers around in my pocket. I would never have told anybody that, nor even allowed myself to think those kinds of thoughts, but deep inside that was where I was. God reminded me of James 4:6 (English Standard Version), "God opposes the proud but gives grace to the humble." No wonder there was no growth and virtually no conversions happening in my church. God was resisting me because of my pride. I had been pursuing ecclesiastical positions in the church, but all along I had been setting myself up to be in line for a denominational position.

God brought me to a fork in my ministry road. There were two paths in front of me. One path led me down the road that God had called me to follow when I was seventeen years old—serving Him as a pastor. The other path led toward denomination positions and status. If I had taken the latter route, I believe if I wanted it enough, God would have allowed my gifts and abilities to succeed in what I was pursuing.

On the other hand, if I chose to serve Him as a pastor, I would see what He could do through me if I fully surrendered to His eternal purposes for my life. God reminded me of the words of the prophet in

Jeremiah 29:11 (NIV), "'For I know the plans I have for you,' declares the Lord, 'plans to prosper you and not to harm you, plans to give you hope and a future.'"

The decision was a no-brainer, and I rededicated myself to serving Him as a pastor. God has demonstrated over and over that His plans are far better than our plans and that His ways are far better than our ways. One of the best decisions I have ever made was abandoning the path toward denominational positions and doing what God created me to do—be a pastor.

In the years since making that decision, I have feared God more than man. The ministry development of The Grace Place since 1993 is linked to being more focused on seeing what God can do and not what Rick can do. The greatest fear I live with is hearing the awesome God of the universe saying, "You wicked, slothful servant" (Matthew 25:26 ESV). I fear that much more than any of the nastiest things ever said about me by the most malicious people I have ever known. When you lead with purpose and direction, not everybody will be thrilled about it, but I have discovered God honors you when you fear Him more than man.

The Fire Within You

Passion is something you either have or do not have. Do not take another leadership step until you have dealt with the issues robbing you of passion for the church, passion for the irreligious people in your community and passion to see the kingdom of God advanced through the ministries of your church. Your church needs a leader who is passionate about ministry. Until there is a fire within that consumes you with a passion to gather all the resources at your disposal to stake out territory that Satan has been controlling, your church will never experience its potential!

I believe that passion is more important than facilities, money, status in the community, or prestige. Until you are passionate about advancing the kingdom, then the kingdom will never advance through your church.

Your church needs a pastor who knows that the reason he exists is to advance the kingdom of Christ through the ministries of the church he serves. If this is your focus, then taking your hands off the plow and abandoning ministry is not an option. You understand that effective ministry is never easy, and that faithfulness during the worst of times and during the best of times is a requirement for effective ministry. If you are going through a tough place in ministry right now, understand that God is testing your commitment to His cause and His kingdom. It is my observation that unbroken servants are of little use to Jesus.

Your church needs a pastor who leads with confidence. You will never have the courage to lead with confidence if you are unsure about whether you ought to be serving in ministry. I have never seen a smaller church transition into a thriving church that did not have a pastor who led with confidence.

It is time to evaluate your attitude toward ministry. Does it reflect an awareness of *"this is what I was born to do"*? Have the disappointments and frustrations of ministry robbed you of the ability to lead with confidence and passion? If you do not know that serving as the pastor of your church is what you were created to do, then I encourage you to allow God to use the rest of this book to challenge you to become consumed with a passion to lead the church of Jesus Christ with all your might and all your strength.

CHAPTER 3

Endurance of a Lion

Lionhearted leaders must develop the heart of a lion. As your church goes through various stages of development, you will quickly discover that ministry leadership is not for the easily intimidated or the faint-hearted. Tremendous blessings come with the development of the church.

At the same time, you will face more massive faith challenges than you would have ever dreamed possible. If someone had told me when we came to The Grace Place Church about the sleepless nights, financial pressures, and disappointments we would experience during each phase of ministry development, I would have thought they were exaggerating! After leading this church for almost three decades now, I have discovered it requires a tremendous amount of resolve, thick skin, lots of grace, and a truckload of courage to advance the kingdom of Christ.

Having said all of that, please don't step back and say, "It just isn't worth it to be a lionhearted leader and be used by God to grow His church. I am going to opt to just be a smaller church pastor." I can tell you the rewards are far greater than the difficulties. There is nothing that thrills me more on a weekend than to see hundreds of people find hope through the power of the gospel of Jesus Christ celebrating God's grace. I get tremendous satisfaction knowing God is working through my life to accomplish kingdom business. Lionhearted pastors understand serving Jesus Christ through the local church is always challenging!

Abandonment

Lionhearted pastors will face the unpleasant reality that there are people you love who either cannot or will not make the journey with you. People come to small churches for a variety of reasons. Sometimes it is because they want to know everybody and believe the church should simply be a big, happy family. When the church grows to three hundred, they suddenly realize they don't know everybody, and the church no longer feels like a happy family to them. Then people you have invested in, shared with, and loved will say, *"I don't feel comfortable here anymore,"* and they will abandon you. Fortunately, many people will make the journey with you, but be prepared for some to eventually leave when their comfort zone gets messed up. They will either look for another small church, or they will begin to attack you because you are the one who is "changing everything" that seemed comfortable and familiar.

Every time the church gets to a new level, many new people join, but another group leaves because the church just crossed the threshold of their comfort zone. I hate losing people, but it's an unfortunate reality that lionhearted leaders must learn to deal with as they lead the church forward.

As I have led The Grace Place through our various transitions, it has been necessary to develop a thicker skin and the ability to allow trivial issues to roll off my back. When a negative situation comes up, I realize how much my scar tissue has grown over the years.

Had the same scenario occurred early in my ministry, it would have bothered me for days or even weeks. Today I let those go a little faster and easier—I give them only a casual response and typically don't think about them again. Please don't get the idea that I am calloused toward people. Time, experience, and the big picture have enabled me to understand that some of the problems that would really upset me years ago are relatively small. The bigger your boat gets, the harder it is for things to rock it.

Negatites

Over the years I have had a number of mentors. Some are pastors; others are successful businessmen. One of my business mentors was a man named Sherm Swenson. Sherm spent his entire business career with Dayton-Hudson Corporation. He started as a stock boy when he was very young, and then moved into various positions of responsibility in different divisions of the company. He finished his business career as the CEO of B. Dalton Books, served on President Reagan's literacy council, and much more. After retiring as a rather young man, he served for about a decade as the leader of non-academic development for a Christian college and seminary in the Midwest.

Sherm and I met many times, and he poured tremendous wisdom, knowledge, and experience into my life. Sherm was a deeply dedicated follower of Jesus Christ and loved the church intensely. From time to time, Sherm talked to me about watching out for "negatites," a word he invented to describe negative, divisive, and difficult people. He would tell me, "Rick, those people will destroy you, the church, and anything and anyone else they can influence." Sherm was so right, and I have seen irreparable damage done to pastors and to churches by "negatites."

Over time, I have heard some malicious words said about me. When people say mean things about you, it is always hard to handle. Every time I start feeling abused, God reminds of Apostle Paul's experiences in ministry. He describes his experiences in 2 Corinthians 11:23–29 (MSG):

I've worked much harder, been jailed more often, beaten up more times than I can count, and at death's door time after time. I've been flogged five times with the Jews' thirty-nine lashes, beaten by Roman rods three times, pummeled with rocks once. I've been shipwrecked three times and immersed in the open sea for a night and a day. In hard traveling year in and year out, I've had to ford rivers, fend off robbers, struggle with friends, struggle with foes. I've been at risk in the city, at risk in the country, endangered by desert sun and sea storm, and betrayed by those I thought were my brothers. I've known drudgery and hard labor, many a long and lonely night without sleep, many a missed meal, blasted by the cold, naked to the weather. And that's not the half of it, when you throw in the daily pressures and anxieties of all the churches.

Half the places Paul went, they were stoning him, whipping him, or beating him with rods before he left town. When I look at the most malicious things that have ever happened to me, they pale in comparison to what he went through.

If you expect long-haul or lionhearted ministry to be about affirmation, encouragement, and positive experiences, you will bail out quickly. Of course, pastors hurt just like everyone else does. Paul felt every stone that hit him and every lash of the three scourgings he experienced. Did it distract him from his vision and focus? Absolutely not. There are people who see it as their mission in life to hurt you, hinder you; and frustrate you. You will never be able to lead for the long haul until your commitment to ministry is greater than last weekend's criticism. God will never bless you with greater ministry opportunities and responsibilities until you have the courage to deal with these issues and not be distracted by them.

Leadership Risks

Being a lionhearted leader requires *taking faith steps into the unknown.* Hebrews 11 is known as "Faith's Hall of Fame." In it, you find many Old Testament men praised for their faith. It was faith that enabled Noah to work for one hundred years to build a ship to avoid a flood— even though he had never seen a single drop of rain! It was faith that enabled Abraham to leave his home in Ur of the Chaldeans to go to a land of promise and spend the rest of his life living in a tent, never realizing in a personal way what God had promised him. It was faith that enabled Moses to see beyond the power of Egypt to a divine responsibility to deliver the people of God to the Promised Land—even though he would never set foot there himself. None of these spiritual giants had any idea what the outcomes would be, other than the fact that God promised to be with them, guide them, protect them, and, ultimately, help them to triumph. If you want to be a long-haul leader, you must be willing to take steps of faith that involve not knowing the ultimate outcomes other than that God will show you the way through. It is scary at times, but there is no advancement of the kingdom in the cocoon of safety.

One of the most ridiculous trends in America today is putting warning labels on virtually everything. It started with cigarettes, and while I think that was a good idea, there are now warnings *everywhere.* You ge and the warning label states, "Consult your doctor first." It comes from this desire to have a risk-free society. America has been the land of opportunity. It is now becoming the land of safety first, where we want to remove all the risks of living. People want cradle-to-grave security.

That is a warning sign because, as the eminent historian Arnold Poynby said, "The heartbeat of a civilization is its spirit of adventure." When safety becomes the number one goal, civilizations historically begin to decline rather than develop. What is true of civilizations is also true of leadership. When safety becomes your number one goal in the church, decline is inevitable. If you are going to be a long-haul pastor, you will discover that your ministry will be composed of a series of risks.

Fear is one of the realities church leaders deal with. On several occasions I have shared with our church this little thought—when fear comes in the front door of my life, faith goes out the back door. When faith comes in the front door, fear goes out the back door. Having said that, I will tell you the lionhearted pastor will deal with the constant temptation to fear.

When fear overrides faith, it paralyzes your leadership potential. It limits your effectiveness and causes you to miss God-given opportunities. Fear keeps us from doing *more* with our lives to fulfill our dreams. Paul Tournier says, "All of us have reservoirs of full potential, vast areas of great satisfaction. But the roads that lead to those reservoirs are guarded by the dragon of fear."

After I finished my ministry training, my wife, Karon, and I moved from Florida to northern Michigan to begin our ministry. I rented a U-Haul truck to move our furniture. That was during the oil crisis in the late 1970s. When we rented the truck, I did not know that it had a governor on the engine so it would not go faster than forty-five miles per hour. A sixteen-hundred-mile trip at forty-five miles per hour is unbearable for a Type A person like me! There were times I thought we were never going to get to Michigan. Fear is kind of like that; it is a governor on your life, and it keeps you from doing what God wants you to do. Fear kept the children of Israel out of the Promised Land for forty years. Because they were afraid of the giants in the land, they spent forty years wandering around in the wilderness.

Many pastors and churches have wandered in a wilderness of ineffectiveness for decades because they are controlled by their fears rather than by their faith. Right after Jesus was crucified, the disciples were locked in a room because of fear. "On the evening of that day, the first day of the week, the doors being locked where the disciples were for fear of the Jews, Jesus came and stood among them and said to them, "Peace be with you" (John 20:19 ESV). Fear locks the doors from the inside. It is a self-imposed prison.

Fear will sabotage your future success. The ancient patriarch Job was a man who let his fears sabotage his future. Job 3:25 (NIV) tells us that when everything was going extremely well for Job, he would find himself fearing he would lose it all. He says, "Everything I fear, and dread comes true." Fear can be a self-fulfilling prophecy. How many times have you had something happen and you have said, "I was afraid this would happen!" The Bible says, "As a man thinks, so is he." Lionhearted pastors know that if they focus on their fears, they are setting themselves up for failure.

Lionhearted leaders focus on their *opportunities* rather than their *obstacles*. Focusing on opportunities enables you to see what God wants you to do. When Joshua and Caleb, Old Testament men of faith, went into the Promised Land to spy and check it out, they saw what they believed God wanted to give them. They saw a land that was overflowing with milk and honey. They saw vineyards they knew God wanted to give them. They saw farms and villages and herds they knew God would give to them.

To see God work in a supernatural way, you must see what He wants to give you and then have the faith to believe He will. After Israel went into the Promised Land, even though he was eighty years old, Caleb, the spy who gave a good report, believed God would give him his mountain. When you focus on your opportunities, you will live with a sense of purpose and meaning in your life. You will have the continual assurance that God is leading you.

Joseph is another biblical example of someone who went through extremely challenging times, but he had a vision of God doing tremendous things through his life. In a couple of dreams God revealed He had a great work for Joseph to carry out. Joseph was able to endure his Egyptian difficulties because he had a clear vision of what God had in store for him. He did not see a slave's garment; instead, he saw the coat of a ruler. He did not see his prison; he saw ahead to palaces and influence! Long-haul pastors can see beyond current challenges and realize that, through them, God is opening a great door of opportunity.

Lionhearted leaders focus on God instead of the opposition. Many pastors, CEOs, and churches are so consumed by their problems they cannot see the God-given opportunities all around them! If you really believe that God is in total control of everything, that He is truly all-powerful, then focus on finding His solution. Do not focus on the opposition. Focusing on the sovereignty of God is key when facing times of intense opposition in ministry.

Many times, I have told God that I could not see a way through the problems, whether financially, building projects, or staffing issues.

I have reminded God that the church belongs to Him, I belong to Him, and if He doesn't come through, we are all in a mess. Every time I have prayed that prayer, God has come through and reminded me this is an "only God" thing. Only when we shift our focus from the horizontal problems of life to the vertical solutions of God's provisions do we see the answers. If you are constantly focusing on the opposition instead of our awesome God, then you are in deep trouble. God has a way through the situation you are dealing with right now!

Long-haul leaders are always ready to seize God-given opportunities. When you act on your faith, God will reward you in an abundant way. God tells us, "Now to him who is able to do far more abundantly than all that we ask or think, according to the power at work within us (Ephesians 3:20 ESV). Don't limit God's blessings by your little faith. God wants to help you to conquer gigantic challenges to reap great rewards. You will also discover that God's promises are trustworthy. He will do what He says He will do.

A lionhearted leader is not "faint of heart." It takes courage and determination to lead the church. Listen to the troubles Apostle Paul says his pastor-leader challenges got him into:

> In fact, in everything we do we try to show that we are true ministers of God. We patiently endure suffering and hardship and trouble of every kind. We have been beaten, put in jail, faced angry mobs, worked to exhaustion, stayed awake through sleepless nights of watching, and gone without food. We have proved ourselves to be what we claim by our wholesome lives and by our understanding of the gospel and by our patience. We have been kind and truly loving and filled with the Holy Spirit ... We stand true to the Lord whether others honor us or despise us, whether they criticize us or commend us. We are honest, but they call us liars. The world ignores us, but we are known to God; we live close to death, but here we are, still very much alive. We have been injured but kept from death. Our hearts ache, but at the same time we have the joy of

the Lord. We are poor, but we give rich spiritual gifts to others. We own nothing, and yet we enjoy everything. (2 Corinthians 6:4–10 Living Bible)

When I look at what Paul dealt with to see the gospel of Jesus Christ prevail in parts of the world that had never heard the life-changing message we are entrusted to share, it is obvious that lionhearted ministry is not for the faint-hearted.

CHAPTER 4

"Can Do, Will Do, Make Do"

Lionhearted leaders understand their attitude has more influence than the words they say. For more than four decades of serving as a pastor and having deep conversations with hundreds of fellow pastors, I have concluded that many have more excuses for doing nothing than the proverbial "Carter has liver pills." They say the reason their church is not growing goes back decades to something that happened, and the church got a bad name in the community, or that people just aren't "interested in spiritual things anymore," or that they have "tried everything and nothing works." Lionhearted pastors will always stand up in that kind of situation and say, "we can do it, we will do it, and to do it we will just make do." Solomon puts it this way in Ecclesiastes 11:4 (New Living Translation): "If you wait for perfect conditions, you will never get anything done."

Lionhearted pastors will always focus on what I call the "can do, will do, make do" approach in every situation. When I am with a pastor who is constantly talking about his limitations and liabilities, I know he is blind to his opportunities. Even the largest and most prosperous churches have limitations on what they can do. Most churches do not have the ultimate in facilities, staff, resources, or location. Your attitude will either paralyze you into total inactivity, or it will help you understand that developing a can-do, will-do, make-do attitude is essential!

Can Do

The lionhearted leader is always going to shift the focus to what he or she *can do*. You will never be able to advance your church until you start looking at your options and opportunities instead of your limitations. No matter how limited or challenging your ministry circumstances are, if we were to spend time together at your place of ministry, I guarantee you we would discover there are a lot of things you *can do*.

My can-do attitude was developed very early in my life by circumstances over which I had no control. My dad was killed in an automobile accident caused by an intoxicated driver. Dad was the pastor of a smaller church, and when he died in 1969, his salary was around a hundred dollars per week. I am the oldest of five children and was fourteen years old when the accident occurred. My dad left no savings, had a $2,000 life insurance policy and left a family of five children for my mother to support. Because of our financial limitations, I immediately began working every day. In those kinds of circumstances, you learn early on to focus on what you can do. When that is your focus, you discover there are all kinds of options available.

When we came to Stuart, the facilities were in sad shape. They consisted of two buildings that were approximately forty feet wide by eighty feet long. One building was the worship center; the other building was primarily occupied by our weekday preschool and secondarily occupied by the church on the weekends. Neither building had been maintained very well. The worship center had no bathrooms (you had to walk through the rain to the preschool building), one office for the secretary, and a nursery, which we converted into my office after we arrived. The whole place had been neglected for fifteen years. There was not a single folding table or chair that did not need to be thrown away and replaced. The carpet was moldy and had holes in it, and the walls were dirty with rust running down to the baseboards.

The attitude of the church was summed up in the words of one board member. About a month after we arrived, we were having a conversation about the possibility of remodeling the worship center, and he said, "Rick, what can you do with this place except tear it down?" Well, we remodeled it then, and we have remodeled it several more times for different uses. It can now continue to serve The Grace Place ministries for another thirty to fifty years—this with a building that could only be torn down in the eyes of a man who did not have a can-do vision.

There is so much you can do if you develop a can-do philosophy of ministry. Since you will never find the perfect church with perfect conditions and perfect people, quit focusing on your liabilities and start focusing on your incredible opportunities. Many of us waste a tremendous amount of time wishing for everything to be different instead of focusing on what we can do, which, ironically, will make things different. I encourage you to start right now making a list of things you can do.

Will Do

A lot of pastors have no problem seeing what they can do. Their challenge is to transition from seeing what they can do to doing something about it. Abraham Lincoln once said he had all kinds of men who were "willing to shed the last drop of their blood for the cause." His problem was finding men who would shed the first drop of blood.

That conversation with the board member would not have

accomplished anything had I not been willing to put some sweat and elbow grease into doing something about it. The *will-do* part of this equation meant that I had to find the financial resources, find the people with the skills to do the work, and set a time to tear the buildings apart and put them back together again. I had to have a willingness to roll up my sleeves, get my hammer and saw out, and work longer and harder on the project than anyone else. Because of the will-do approach, the remodeling project was completed in a matter of weeks, and the positive impact on the church was immediate and dynamic.

The will-do issue was a major factor in the stagnation The Grace Place had experienced for over a decade prior to our arrival. During a twelve-year period, at least a half dozen plans had been presented to the church with great fanfare, but nothing ever materialized. So, people began to think nothing would ever happen. When we talked about this project and then completed it, people began to believe change would happen. In fact, it was not long until I was getting consistent feedback like, "If Rick talks about it, you better watch out because it is going to happen."

Long-haul pastors know they will seriously discredit themselves and the church by talking about things that never materialize. Be incredibly careful about discussing ideas, projects, and ministries before you have done enough homework on them to know whether they can be accomplished.

A great example of a will-do attitude is found in the Old Testament prophet Nehemiah. He was a leader who knew facilitating positive change required taking personal responsibility. Nehemiah accepted personal responsibility for the negative circumstances in Jerusalem. In Nehemiah 1:3 (NIV), he says, "Those who survived the exile and are back in the province are in great trouble and disgrace. The wall of Jerusalem is broken down and its gates have been burned with fire."

He could have dismissed the report and said, "Too bad, what a tragic ending for the once glorious city of David." He could have said, "I am cupbearer in Persia now, and my career and destiny are here. Besides, what can one man do?" But instead, Nehemiah had a will-do attitude, came to Jerusalem, and started rebuilding the walls, gathering a team to help.

Lionhearted leaders like Nehemiah do not hesitate to take on responsibility. I know pastors who always pass the buck, expecting someone else to take the reins of leadership, someone else to do their dirty work. If we do not have a will-do attitude, we are dramatically limiting our leadership potential and the church we serve.

Nehemiah teaches us that persistence pays off. "So the wall was completed on the twenty-fifth of Elul, in fifty-two days. When all our enemies heard about this, all the surrounding nations were afraid and lost their self-confidence, because they realized that this work had been done with the help of God" (Nehemiah 6:15–16 NIV). A will-do attitude enables you to stay with the job until it is completed. Nehemiah is an inspiration to leaders everywhere because he stayed with the renovation project until it was finished. Lionhearted leaders change their churches and powerfully impact the lives of people when they are not intimidated by the challenges they face. They just have a will-do attitude toward getting the job done.

Effective pastors and leaders also understand the difference between putting in time and getting the job done. So many pastors do not understand that putting in a day at the office does not equal getting the job done. While in both high school and college, my brothers and I worked together hanging and finishing drywall. We were able to make excellent money if we worked hard and long. Because we were paid by the number of sheets of drywall we hung in a house and would not get paid until the job was completed, I learned to look at an assignment as something to finish.

I know pastors who will talk about how many hours they work each week. I am never impressed with the number of hours a person works; instead, I want to know what was accomplished. At the same time, church leaders question what these pastors were getting done. Will-do pastors are far more focused on what they are accomplishing than the hours they are putting in on the job.

Take a moment and evaluate projects, ministries, and objectives you have planned but have not taken the steps to start or finish. Lionhearted pastors rise to the challenges in front of them and understand, no matter what the opposition, that victory will come if they just finish the job!

Make Do

We do not live in a perfect world, and there are times when getting the job done requires *making do*. I like cars and have a Dodge Charger Scat Pac and a 1990 GMC truck I have restored. I enjoy tinkering with them and have done so most of my life. When you work on a car, there will be times when you need a wrench that you just do not have in your toolbox. Necessity is the mother of invention and, if you are like me, you will make do by heating up one of the other wrenches with your torch and bending it so that it will work. It is not ideal, but it gets the job done and the vehicle back on the road.

It really is no different in ministry. You may be aware of an area of tremendous ministry need but simply do not have the personnel to develop that ministry the way you wish it could be done. Lionhearted pastors with a make-do philosophy will figure out how to respond to that need, even when the circumstances, facility, or assigned leader is not ideal.

We have had a unique chemistry with The Grace Place, and God's blessing has been very evident from the first weekend until the present. There has also been this attitude *can do, will do, and make do* as well.

The easiest way for me to illustrate this is with another building story. Within a year of completing the chapel remodeling project I talked about earlier, it became apparent we were going to need additional facilities. We started a second service on Sundays, and that helped, but with the growth patterns we were experiencing, it was evident to the elders and me that a building project was necessary. We began praying about this need and, at the same time, putting together plans. In the summer of 1994, we raised $10,000, which was a huge amount of money for the church at the time, to hire an architect. The architect ultimately put together concept plans that we could not use because the building he designed was too expensive. That got us started on the track toward looking for a God solution.

Within a brief time, we became aware that Pratt and Whitney Corporation had some modular commercial buildings they were donating to churches. Some of the buildings were 180 feet wide by 250 feet deep. After discussing it, the elders made the decision to acquire sixteen thousand square feet of these buildings, and we moved them to our site in late 1995. We called this facility our Ministry Center, and its renovation was completed in November 1996.

Some churches looked at the buildings, but only a few responded to the offer. The primary reason other churches turned away from them was because of a built-in limitation—the ceilings were only eight feet high. Most pastors looked at the low ceilings and said, "We can't do anything with those buildings." They then returned to their limited facilities and did more laps around the same track, not realizing they had just missed the opportunity of their lives. We looked at the same buildings and said, "This is how we will make do." We were able to gain an additional eighteen inches over the stage area, install television monitors into special recessed areas we built into the attic spaces, and install TV cameras that made it possible for everyone to see, no matter where they sat. When we were through, it was such a dramatic improvement over what we previously had; it felt like the church had moved into the Taj Mahal.

The impact of the can-do, will-do, make-do approach has been dramatic. We took what other people did not want and made do with it, and God blessed us in incredible ways. The Ministry Center was completed in November 1996. By that time, the church had grown to 290 attendees with two services in the chapel building. In May 2002, we moved out of the Ministry Center facility into our new $3.5 million Celebration Center. In five and half years, the church had grown to 750 attendees with three services. God will honor a church that has a can-do, will-do, make-do philosophy.

I am concerned, as our facilities grow bigger and better, and we can do more with them, we do not lose the attitude of doing the maximum with what we have, or even more. From time to time, I talk to our senior staff and staff pastors about not losing the "can-do, will-do, make-do" philosophy that has brought us to where we are and will take us to places we have not yet gone.

When I was growing up, my parents were concerned about the kind of language we used. If they ever caught one of us using inappropriate language, we knew there was a consequence that we would not like.

Lionhearted leaders always make sure they *clean up their language*. We are not talking about foul language here, but about words you need to wash out of your vocabulary because they have a way of destroying

Richard H. Addison Jr.

the can do, will do, make do philosophy we have been discussing. They are words like *try, can't,* and *won't.* These words have a devastating impact on your attitude toward both challenges and opportunities. I have yet to see anyone overcome a challenge by *trying* to do something about it, by telling themselves they *can't* do anything about it, or they *won't* do anything about it.

Lionhearted pastors understand there are no impossibilities with our God who has absolutely no limitations on His resources, wisdom, strength, and power. When you focus on God's resources, you will be a can-do, will-do, make-do leader! You will become a person God can work through to help His church prevail against the very gates of hell!

CHAPTER 5

Manage Yourself

Lionhearted pastors all seem to have the ability to manage themselves in the vital areas of life and ministry. Words like mature, self-disciplined, productive, stable, ethical, etc. describe their nature. Managing yourself is not just being self-disciplined (though that is involved); it is learning to be your own boss, requiring yourself to do the right things, keeping on task, managing your time well, and developing a strong work ethic.

It only makes sense that if you are going to be able to manage others (that is what happens when you hire staff), you must first learn to manage yourself. All my life I have been an astute observer of other people. I noticed early on that the people who rose to the top and stayed there in any organization had this common characteristic. They first learned to manage themselves—their emotions, their reactions, their attitudes, their time, their money, their priorities, and their habits.

Most pastors start their ministry in smaller churches and develop some bad habits. I have hired a few pastors who have only worked in little churches. Many of them have never learned to work "regular" hours. I discovered that many of them were accustomed to fooling around half the morning, or maybe for an entire day, and then told themselves they would make it up by working late. Unfortunately, most of them would be fired in less than a week if they were working in any other job. Because of those poor work habits, you never knew when they were going to show up and when they were going to disappear.

Since observing these kinds of poor work practices, I have concluded that the church will never make the kind of impact God wants her to until and unless we pastors learn better practices of self-management and give the church the best of our energy and efforts. God has never honored carelessness, casualness, or disorganization. Proverbs has strong things to say about this attitude: Lazy men are soon poor; hard workers get rich. (Proverbs 10:4 TLB). If you want to be a lionhearted pastor who God uses in a positive and powerful way, then learning to manage yourself is vital.

One of the basic realities of life is that either you manage yourself or someone else will manage you. I have discovered that Rick Addison will make Rick Addison work harder than any boss has ever been able to do. To become a lionhearted pastor, become your own boss and require yourself to accomplish the things that really matter in life and ministry. Managing yourself means you are a self-starter, disciplined, more focused on finishing the task than on how long it takes to do it, will do the right thing whether everyone knows it or not, and are motivated by a God-inspired passion to use your one and only life to make the maximum impact on as many people as possible.

Each year I teach a class for men based on Gene Getz's book *The Measure of a Man*. I use the class to disciple men and prepare them for potential leadership in our church. The book looks at each of the twenty different qualities of a spiritual leader that Paul identifies in 1 Timothy 3 and Titus 1. Each of those characteristics of a spiritually mature person is distinct, and yet they are interwoven together to produce the overarching value of a person who is *"above reproach."* Without those qualities being built into our lives, if we are placed in positions of spiritual leadership in the church, we will self-destruct.

Managing yourself is really a character issue. If you are unreliable in your schedule, there is a high probability you will be unreliable in other areas of your life. Years ago, I was talking with someone who told me his pastor was a liar. His statement caught me off guard because I thought I knew his pastor. He went on to say, "He makes appointments with people and doesn't keep them, or he tells people he will take care of something for them and then never does it. Every time anyone says anything about these issues, his standard response is 'I forgot.'" Sometime later I had the opportunity to work a little closer with this pastor and discovered that not only was he sloppy in his schedule; he also consistently misled me, told partial truths, and proved to be exactly what I was told—he was a liar and even worse, a cheat. You cannot lead people to places you have not gone; personality and charisma will take you only so far. Lionhearted leaders understand character is the only thing that will enable them to endure for the long haul.

Managing Your Emotions

Emotions are a part of being human. It is inevitable that we are going to have times where we feel better than others. Some circumstances we go through take a huge emotional toll on us. Some people are dramatically affected by their emotions. If they are feeling good and having a good day, everyone knows it! On the other hand, if they are not feeling good, and their day is not going very well, everyone knows it! Lionhearted pastors know they cannot be mastered by their emotions—that God alone will give them the strength and courage to be the master of their emotions.

If we do not master our emotions, those we influence with our leadership have no idea which person they are dealing with on any given day. The unpredictability of the pastor who is mastered by his emotions will cause the church and staff to become frustrated and distrustful.

Early in my ministry I had the experience of working with someone like that. When I had a meeting with this person there was no predicting whether I would be treated warmly or like I had a contagious disease. He made me either feel like a winner or a complete loser, depending on the mood he was in. After a few years of dealing with his emotional roller coaster I lost all respect for him and did everything I could to avoid being around him. Ultimately, it was his undoing as a leader!

If we do not master our emotions, the people around us, who will usually try to constantly prop us up emotionally and encourage us, will suffer. We had a staff member like that, and if he came in emotionally down, then it affected more than just him because several staff members would have to drop everything they were doing and take hours trying to encourage him and lift him. After this happened repeatedly, I had a conversation with him and pointed out how selfish his emotional instability really was. I called him by name and said, "When you are having a bad day, you are not satisfied until you are making sure other people are as well." He did not like it, but it was profoundly true. The most unselfish thing you can do is to make sure you are allowing God to master your emotions, so that others are not being negatively affected or influenced by it.

Lionhearted pastors lead their church with a steady hand and know that no matter what their personal issues are, they must not let their emotions interfere with their leadership responsibilities. Many years ago, our youngest son developed an alcohol addiction, and we have dealt with many challenging situations because of it. The first time he came home drunk was on a Saturday afternoon. His brother called me and said that he had passed out in the entryway to our house. Our first weekend service was that Saturday evening, so I was at the church, and it was just a little over an hour until the service was to start. I went home, and it was worse than my wife and I could imagine.

I got to the church a few minutes before the service started and desperately prayed for God to help me to minister to those who were there. My administrative assistant told me after the service she had no idea how I held it together for that service. I told her it wasn't me—it was God helping me. After the service I left the church, and Karon and I went to the parking lot outside of the jail and sat in our car and cried until we did not have any more tears. It felt like my heart was being ripped out of my chest. I am not telling you this is what you should do in a similar situation, but all of us deal with emotional trauma. If we allow Him, God will help us not to put our church on an emotional roller coaster because of what is going on personally in our lives.

Managing Your Attitude

Lionhearted pastors understand that life and ministry are unfair. It is not what happens to us that is the issue; it's what happens in us that is the real issue. When I let injustice, betrayal, abandonment, or anything else become a root of bitterness in my heart, I will invariably struggle with my attitude. I cannot count the conversations I have had with pastors who have allowed themselves to be negative, cynical, and vindictive because of the negative situations that have happened to them.

In the beatitudes Jesus says, "Blessed are the merciful, for they will be shown mercy" (Matthew 5:7 NIV). Obviously, to be merciful means that someone has taken advantage of you. I do not have a difficult time showing mercy to those who are affirming and loving me. But we need to show mercy to the treacherous people who are trying to destroy us. In the Lord's Prayer, Jesus says, "Forgive us the wrongs we have done, as we forgive the wrongs that others have done to us" (Matthew 6:12 TEV).

Jesus teaches us that refusing to forgive those who have wronged

37

us has a tragic effect on our attitudes. When we refuse to forgive for an extended period, we will become an embittered person who only sees the negative and cannot see the positive because our bitterness blinds us to the light.

When you refuse to forgive, you are always focused on the past, and you cannot have an attitude of anticipation of good and wonderful things when you're looking backward. God tells us repeatedly that he *has hope for us!* "For I know the plans I have for you," declares the LORD, "plans to prosper you and not to harm you, plans to give you hope and a future" (Jeremiah 29:11 NIV).

The Bible tells us that God loves to take the burned-up ashes of our lives and bring unbelievable beauty out of them. None of that happens when we are wrapped up in a blanket of anger, bitterness, hate, and revenge toward people who have wronged us in some way. I've heard it said the "the same sun that hardens clay, softens wax." When we begin to understand the unpayable debt of sin, of which we have been forgiven, it will transform how we forgive others.

In the parable of the unmerciful servant, Jesus teaches us that when we compare how much God has forgiven us of the worst thing anyone has done to us, it is virtually nothing compared to the unpayable debt we have been forgiven. A lionhearted leader knows he must consistently practice forgiving others if he is going to have the positive and forward-focused attitude God wants us to have.

Lionhearted pastors know merely thinking positive thoughts will not necessarily give them a positive attitude. The Bible repeatedly tells us our attitude is shaped by having a faith-focus in the God who will do what He says He will do.

Far too many times I have looked at a problem, and my immediate reaction was that it was too big, too complex, and too expensive. When I look at my problems through the prism of my resources, my abilities, and my experiences, it is inevitable I will become negative and discouraged. Lionhearted pastors know our God doesn't have the words *impossible, too complicated*, and *too expensive* in His vocabulary. In fact, if you have a printed dictionary at your house or office, I challenge you to take a razor knife and physically cut out those words from your dictionary. Repeatedly I have asked God to stop me whenever one of those words slips out of my mouth. The Bible reminds us that what comes out of our mouths is evidence of what is going on in our hearts.

Every time the lionhearted leader encounters situations that seem to be impossible, he will go to the Bible and find one of God's promises that addresses the situation and claim that promise as God's word of assurance. The Bible reminds us that God loves to do things that humans find impossible. Every time God has turned something around, it is because of someone claiming a promise for what looks to be impossible to see what only God can do.

One time after a promise was fulfilled, I had person after person in our church say to me, "Rick, only God!"

If we could spend a half hour together talking about your ministry, your life, and your experiences, I could tell you how things were going to go for the most part in your ministry and life for the next five to ten years. If you are bitter, cynical, and negative, then you are focused on the past, and you are either stuck where you are or are regressing. If you share your experiences, both the good and the bad, if you are forgiving and redemptive in your attitude, if you share some promises God has given to you, then it does not really matter what you have gone through; God has amazing things planned for you. You really do have a hope and a future!

Managing Your Reactions

One of the great tests of managing yourself is the wisdom to manage your reactions. Everyone in ministry deals with people. Often, I will remind our ministry staff to always remember first and foremost that we are in the "people business."

Most of the people we work and interact with are wonderful, caring, loving, and supportive. On the other hand, there are those who think it is their God-given prerogative to be critical, negative, reactive, and angry. When you are dealing with people like that it is to be expected they are going to make remarks that are hurtful, malicious, and frequently very un-Christlike. It's easy to allow our emotions to overcome wisdom and respond in a like manner.

Over the years I have learned that to respond to a hurtful statement quickly means I will inevitably have to go and apologize for what I said in response. Over the past twenty years or so as the internet has become an integral part of our lives, many people have resorted to rashly sending hurtful emails or text messages. For most of us, our initial reaction is to fire back an angry response. Always remember those emails and text messages are easily forwarded, copied, and then sent to others who are not involved in the problem, and a huge battle can develop almost immediately. I have learned that many of the people who are so "mighty with a computer mouse" are cowards face-to-face. My standard response to others who want to engage is "obviously we need to talk," and then I will let them know when I am available. Most of the time they will decide the issue is not important enough to meet with and discuss in person.

If I get upset over what someone is or is not doing, whether staff or in the church, I have learned it is always best to wait for twenty-four hours to respond. I have a strong personality, and without trying I can be intimidating. Sometimes I will tell my assistant to make sure I do not have any scheduled or impromptu meetings with that person for at least one day.

If you want to be a lionhearted leader, never use the pulpit or stage to make a point that is directed toward a person who has you upset about something. To me, that is being an on-stage coward who is using their platform to ventilate their frustration, or even worse, to strike back at the person at whom they are angry.

Managing Your Ministry Priorities

When I was in high school, I learned the drywall trade, and at age sixteen I was subcontracting drywall jobs and running my own crew. I continued running this subcontracting business through my last two years of high school and through my college years. Fortunately, I was able to make a lot of money by 1970s standards, and both my wife I graduated from college debt free.

I learned a lot from those early years of subcontracting that helped me immensely in our ministry journey. I learned that hard work pays off, that there is a direct link between productivity and compensation, and that to get the projects completed on time I had to establish priorities.

Many pastors are sabotaging themselves and shortening their ministry opportunities because they cannot distinguish what needs to be done from what should be done when they have the time. My top priority is to make sure I am well prepared for the weekend services, both the sermon and our worship planning. That is why I go to our house in Alabama about every two months and spend a week working on sermons, praying, and analyzing the needs of our people. This helps me to be focused on the priority of preaching, and it makes a huge difference to get away and be able to spend days concentrating on what

I am going to be speaking about for the next few months. It also helps our worship ministries to be more focused and creative in preparing for our weekend services.

A second-level priority is shepherding and pastoral care. As a result, I spend a good deal of time ministering to people one on one. To do that, it is essential to use a calendar consistently. The very needy people want to absorb as much of your time as they can. Make sure you know Christian counselors in your area so you can refer those people to someone else. Don't let someone else's crisis become your crisis. I have had people call and tell me their spouse just left them. If I can meet with them quickly I will, but many times they have seen this coming, and they have buried their head in the sand like the proverbial ostrich, pretending I can make it all go away.

I have other priorities (obviously keeping my relationship with God number one and my relationship with my spouse number two). I believe those are already understood. I am talking about keeping your ministry priorities straight. Knowing what your priorities are will keep you focused and on track. You will know it, your staff will know it, and your church will as well.

Managing Your Time

Lionhearted pastors know that time is their most treasured resource. If you lose your money, with wise adjustments you can recover what was lost, but when you lose your time, it is gone forever. Somewhere at the midpoint of life you notice that something very subtle starts to happen to you. Instead of thinking of all the years you have in front of you, you start thinking about the number of years you have left. When you are in your younger years it seems that life stretches out in front of you like a never-ending path, and many people never think during those years of using their time wisely.

Because my dad died when he was just thirty-nine years old, I have lived with the awareness that there are no guarantees of life being this unending path in front of me. I am sure this has contributed to me wanting to live every day to its maximum. That does not mean I have not wasted time, but never for an extended period.

Lionhearted pastors also know the importance of making the main thing the main thing. For me, the main thing is knowing that I am in the right place and doing the right things while I am here. It is taking the gifts of the Spirit—my natural God-given gifts and talents—and developing them to their maximum potential.

My calling is to be the pastor of a local church, and for those reasons I have not pursued a lot of outside speaking engagements unless they have a multiplication component built into them. If I can share some of what I have learned and am learning in ministry with people who are serving as pastors or are preparing to be pastors, then that is worth my time and energy. In fact, that is why I am taking the time to write this book. Other than that, I have very little interest in going somewhere and speaking just because I can. My heart is in the local church and in investing in the lives of people I love and serve. It seems like every time I have spoken somewhere else, I ask myself, *Why would I leave The Grace Place to come here and preach?* I know what my calling is and where it is, and that is where I want to be.

All pastors should have a time management tool that does more than collect dust on their desk. It should guide them through the day. Many pastors are notoriously sloppy with their calendars and forget their appointments. Over time those sloppy behaviors destroy the pastor's credibility. I now have my assistant call the day before I am scheduled to meet with anyone, including pastors, to remind them of their appointments. Some of the guys I have arranged to meet have forgotten our meetings several times in a row, and after that I refuse to waste my time scheduling anything with them in the future.

Managing our time means that we must learn to work harder and smarter. A lot of people say they just want to work smarter. I say that working smarter always means working harder. Virtually every day I review and update my "to do" list and the items that were not completed the week before and lay them out for each day of the coming week. I use Outlook's Task List feature to do that because it lets me prioritize the list, set up repeated tasks, and schedule tasks out for as far ahead as I can realistically foresee. I have things on my "to do" list that will pop up three or more years down the road. Every evening or early the next morning, I work through the list for the new day, marking completed items on the list and rescheduling uncompleted items. I know that to accomplish anything of significance, I must prioritize my "to do" list daily.

There are times when I feel like a slave to my task list and to my calendar, but by being methodical I can meet more people and manage more projects than the average person does. My administrative assistant arranges most of my appointments, and I am generally scheduled from early in the morning until the end of the day and at a variety of evening events.

Managing Your Personal World

A lionhearted leader knows that managing his personal world is a perquisite to leading and managing the church. Listen to Apostle Paul's instructions to the young pastor Timothy who was the pastor to the church in Ephesus:

He must not be a drunkard or a violent man, but gentle
and peaceful; he must not love money; he must be able
to manage his own family well and make his children
obey him with all respect. For if a man does not know
how to manage his own family, how can he take care of
the church of God? (1 Timothy 3:3–5 TEV)

Apostle Paul makes it clear that if Timothy is to be a godly man,
he must manage his personal world well. The apostle sums up the
importance of all this with the question in 1 Timothy 3:5 NIV: how
can he take care of the church of God if he cannot manage himself and
his personal world? That is why focusing on this issue is so important.

Lionhearted pastors know their public ministry is just a reflection
of their personal devotion to Jesus Christ. Many years ago, I read Bill
Hybel's book *Too Busy Not to Pray.* In the book, Bill challenges readers
to make their personal quiet time the priority of their day. He also
recommended keeping a daily life and prayer journal.

I was very challenged by the book and began putting into practice
the daily life and prayer journal. It has become a regular part of my
personal walk with Jesus and has had a powerful impact on my own
spiritual life. Many times I talk to God in my daily journal about my
fears, injustices, criticisms, and doubts. There I can dump so much of
my frustration and frequently experience God encouraging, comforting,
and strengthening me. This is a very private and very personal thing for
me. I always journal on my computer in a file to which only God and
I know the password. It is so personal and so much between me and
God that if anyone ever attempted to open my journal, I would find it
to be a horrible violation of my life.

If you do not journal that is okay, but for me personally it has been
what God has used repeatedly to minister to my spirit and give me

the special awareness of his presence and peace in my life. The prayer journal is part of my quiet time where I express my devotion to God, confess my sins to him, thank him for his blessings and answers to prayer, and petition him for the needs and concerns in my life. For the past few years, I have put a list of items I am praying about in my journal that I am expecting God to change and transform.

Managing Your Influence

Lionhearted pastors know that managing their personal world in a God-honoring way has tremendous impact on how they influence others. That means they cannot give in to abusing any substances or worshiping any "false idols" or giving in to greed or gluttony or anything that may compromise their integrity as pastors. Apostle Paul, talking to Timothy, says that the spiritual leader "must not be a drunkard" (1 Timothy 3:3 ESV). I am a student of the Bible and am well aware that the Bible does not prohibit the use of alcohol but prohibits drunkenness. At the same time, Apostle Paul also talks about the principle of not eating meat offered to idols in 1 Corinthians 8:4–13:

> So then, about eating the food offered to idols: we know that an idol stands for something that does not really exist; we know that there is only the one God. Even if there are so-called "gods," whether in heaven or on earth, and even though there are many of these "gods" and "lords," yet there is for us only one God, the Father, who is the Creator of all things and for whom we live; and there is only one Lord, Jesus Christ, through whom all things were created and through whom we live. But not everyone knows this truth. Some people have been

so used to idols that to this day when they eat such food, they still think of it as food that belongs to an idol; their conscience is weak, and they feel they are defiled by the food. Food, however, will not improve our relationship with God; we shall not lose anything if we do not eat, nor shall we gain anything if we do eat. Be careful, however, not to let your freedom of action make those who are weak in the faith fall into sin. Suppose a person whose conscience is weak in this matter sees you, who have so-called "knowledge," eating in the temple of an idol; will not this encourage him to eat food offered to idols? And so, this weak person, your brother for whom Christ died, will perish because of your "knowledge"! And in this way, you will be sinning against Christ by sinning against other Christians and wounding their weak conscience. So then, if food makes a believer sin, I will never eat meat again, so as not to make a believer fall into sin. (1 Corinthians 8:4–13 TEV)

Each summer while I was growing up, my family would attend "camp meetings." At those camp meetings, which had three services a day, the ministers would generally preach what I call "hellfire and brimstone" sermons. They also would have youth services for the teens. When I was twelve years old, we were at a camp meeting in Ohio, and I attended my very first youth service. This was back in the late 1960s, and they were showing a black and white reel-to-reel movie on the effects that alcohol has on the human body, in particular the destruction of brain cells that never regenerate themselves when they are destroyed by alcohol. They also talked about its effects on the liver and other vital organs of the human body.

Then they showed a reenactment of an actual accident that occurred between a lifelong alcoholic and a college-aged girl. It showed the alcoholic leaving a bar intoxicated and the girl leaving a party acting foolishly; both affected by alcohol. They were in a crash.

While both were impaired, an autopsy of the brains of both the lifelong alcoholic and the college girl revealed that the older man's brain was smaller and darker, and the girl's was larger and lighter. Over time, alcohol had reduced the cognitive function of the older man. At one point in his life, the man's brain would have looked like that of the seventeen-year-old. However, the years of alcohol abuse led ultimately to his ruin. This visual had a profound impact on me.

That day I decided I would never become an alcoholic, and the only guaranteed way that would happen was to never touch the first drop. Two years later, my dad was killed in a car wreck by an alcoholic, and that permanently sealed the decision for me. This was not a spiritual decision because I did not come into a life-changing relationship with Jesus Christ until five years later. But it was a life-values decision that I have never regretted making. I don't know if I have the genes that would lead me to alcoholism. But I do know I will never have to find out.

As a pastor, I also believe if the people whom I serve see me sitting at a table in one of our restaurants drinking a beer or a glass of wine, they will be tempted to order their own alcoholic drink of choice. For those who are alcoholics, one drink will take them right back into their addiction. A lionhearted pastor does not want to be an obstacle to anyone in their spiritual journey.

First Corinthians 8:9 (NIV) states, "Be careful, however, that the exercise of your rights does not become a stumbling block to the weak."

Personal Hygiene and Appearance

Many times, people have a hard time hearing pastors because of the distractions in their appearance. Remember most of us speak in front of people every weekend for about thirty minutes.

Because many pastors are constantly meeting people for meals (I am one of them), it is easy to start putting on a lot of extra weight. When our weight becomes a distraction, people begin to see us as undisciplined and careless. I remember growing up hearing guys preach who were a hundred or more pounds overweight railing against smoking cigarettes because of the poor Christian witness it gives. But they seemed to be oblivious to the fact the Bible never mentions cigarettes (although I am not for smoking and believe those who smoke are terrible witnesses) but on the other hand repeatedly talks about gluttony.

We had a young man do a ministry internship with us a while back and in my last one-on-one meeting with him I talked to him about how his out-of-control weight would limit his ministry opportunities and people taking him seriously. He knew I was not being hurtful in the way I approached him, and he listened. After his internship he went back to the Christian university he attended and lost around one hundred pounds. Repeatedly I have affirmed him, and he has thanked me several times for helping him to see a huge blind spot in his life.

Many years ago, we had two hurricanes come through our area of South Florida, exactly three weeks apart. Our president at that time was George W. Bush. He discreetly flew into our town and arranged with the American Red Cross to meet with the leaders of the nonprofits that were involved in hurricane relief. I was invited because of the part The Grace Place played in those efforts. Some of our staff were able to join us. When I met him, a few attributes stood out to me about the forty-third president of the United States.

First, President Bush was genuinely thankful for what we were doing in providing relief for those in our area who were so devastated by the storms. Second, he took the time to shake each person's hand and have his picture taken with us. The third thing I noticed was that he had a lot of what I called "geezer hair" in his ears. I have had people say, "you noticed that when you met the president?" My response was: "I couldn't help it." I thought then, surely someone who cuts his hair would at least do something about that but obviously not. If that is distracting for a president, think of how much more distracting it is for us as pastors to not be well-groomed and take care of ourselves.

It is not only important to be aware of our weight; we need to demonstrate a well-ordered life in hygiene and personal grooming. As a guy gets older, he needs to be aware of how distracting "geezer hair" can be and keep everything trimmed and neat. I get my hair cut about every two weeks because I cannot stand to have hundreds of people ask on their way out of church, "You got a haircut?" which means I noticed you looking a little shabby before. Those may seem to be small items, but the difference between okay and excellence is always found in the details.

Managing Your Money Well

Long-haul pastors know managing their money in a God-honoring way is essential. Remember what Apostle Paul tells the young pastor in 1 Timothy 3:4 (ESV): "He must manage his own household well, with all dignity keeping his children submissive." My Bible college president used to say in our chapel services and when he was talking to the ministerial students, "If you cannot pay your bills and be a pastor, then pay your bills." He was telling us that how we manage our money has a tremendous impact on our ability to influence those we lead.

The number of pastors who have lost their ministries because they are constantly broke, borrowing money from people in the church, and not paying their bills is at an epidemic level.

Managing your money means that you avoid debt as much as possible. When Karon and I got married, we decided to avoid as much debt as possible. We got married after our freshman year in college. While students, we faithfully returned God's tithe to him, believing that God's blessing the 90 percent would always go further than 100 percent on our own. The result was that both of us went on and graduated with every school bill paid in full. That was without grants, no assistance from anyone else, and with no loans. When we graduated from Bible college, we did not owe anything on our cars, on furniture, or on anything else. Karon and I worked extremely hard to make that happen. I was doing drywall work, and Karon was cleaning houses. On the wall in my office, I have mounted my old drywall hammer on a plaque with this inscription under it: "Rick and Karon's College Scholarship." Learn to work and never forget "it is always easier to borrow money than to pay it back," as my old granny used to say.

As Christians we have tremendous freedom in Christ, but we should never use that freedom to be a stumbling block to others, and we should always be aware that when we are in leadership, people are watching us very closely.

Many pastors do not seem to understand that the more we gain influence, the fewer rights and freedoms we have. It is an adage, but profoundly true: "You have to give up to go up." Every step up the ladder of influence means we also give up freedom in our lives. God is not able to use many of us in the ways He wants to because we are unwilling to let go of a freedom to gain greater influence. That is why learning to manage yourself is critical if you are going to be a long-haul pastor.

God will use a well-managed life to accomplish great things for His kingdom. It is critically important if you are going to make a maximum impact on those you serve and on your community. Do not let Satan sabotage God's purposes for you by a sloppy life or mismanagement.

CHAPTER 6

Ministry Ethics

Because we live in a culture that since the 1960s has become increasingly secular and focused on removing God from the public areas of American life, the secularization of people serving in ministry is astounding to me. God's absolute values have been replaced by situational ethics. Most people in our culture and in our churches no longer believe that God's values of honesty, morality, sexual integrity, debt repayment, commitment to vows, the permanence of marriage, and business integrity apply to their lives. That is why many Christians and unfortunately many people serving in ministry positions will justify deception, dishonesty, and cheating because that is the easy way out of circumstances they are in.

Ministry ethics seems to have almost disappeared in the last thirty years. Ministry ethics focuses on values, ministry functions, and practices on which we build our ministry. Many of us have succumbed to the influences of our increasingly secular culture. As a result, we are fast losing our ability to maintain ministry ethics, and the church is fragmenting in so many ways that it breaks the heart of a loving God! This fragmenting causes division, slander, gossip, malicious vendettas, and more. In many places these negative practices have become the norm rather than the exception. Many years ago, I heard a great spiritual leader say, "The worst sin a person can commit is to reject the claim of Jesus Christ in their life. But the second worst sin a person can commit is to divide the body of Christ." A clear understanding of the biblical principles of ministry ethics is extremely important.

Far too many spiritual leaders function like God's principles are merely suggestions and have no application to them. Because of those attitudes, church leaders are not building their lives and ministries on the foundations of biblical truth and integrity. Listen to what Jesus says in Revelation 21:8 (NIV): "But the cowardly, the unbelieving, the vile, the murderers, the sexually immoral, those who practice magic arts, the idolaters and all liars—they will be consigned to the fiery lake of burning sulfur. This is the second death."

Always Tell the Truth

My commitment to absolute honesty came from what the Bible says about telling the truth, and those truths were reinforced by my parents backing up that principle with serious consequences. My dad said to me on more than one occasion, "Rick, if you break our rules, you know there will be consequences, but if you break the rules and then lie about it, the consequences will be much worse than if you just go ahead and tell the truth!" I knew my dad meant business, and I did not have to imagine what the consequences would be like if I lied to him. Unfortunately, far too many "spiritual leaders" did not have that kind of father, and they have lived their lives telling lies, half-truths, and misleading statements for so long they do it with no thought of consequences or any sense of guilt.

The ninth commandment says in Exodus 20:16 (NIV): "You shall not give false testimony against your neighbor." Throughout the Bible,

God emphasizes repeatedly the importance of telling the truth, all the time and in all situations. When a staff member misleads me, shades the truth, or tells a half-truth, I can always pick up on their dishonesty. I then find it impossible to trust them. The foundation upon which all relationships remain strong is trust, and when that is gone, there is nothing left upon which to build.

I have discovered that when a staff member is comfortable telling and living a lie, this usually is the gateway into every other sin. If your life is built on the ethic of always telling the truth, it is a great barrier to sexual sin, to financial dishonesty, slander, gossip, exaggeration, etc. Satan knows that if he can bring us to a place of violating this ethic, we are pretty much clay in his hands to do with us whatever he wants. Revelation 21:8 (ESV) says: "But as for the cowardly, the faithless, the detestable, as for murderers, the sexually immoral, sorcerers, idolaters, and all liars, their portion will be in the lake that burns with fire and sulfur, which is the second death." Jesus gives this list of ungodly people and wraps it up with these words: " … and *all liars …*" (emphasis mine); for the rest of the people he refers to them as *"the murderers, the sexually impure …"* (emphasis mine). Out of seven categories of ungodly people, he uses the word *the*, but for the eighth category, liars, it is *all liars*. Jesus is saying that murderers, the sexually impure, vile people, idolaters, all cannot do what they do without simultaneously being liars.

I understand this is a multimillennial old problem. Abraham demonstrated situational ethics as far back as four thousand years ago when he said that Sarah was his sister and was going to let the pagan king rape her just to save his own neck.

> Abraham moved from Mamre to the southern part of Canaan and lived between Kadesh and Shur. Later, while he was living in Gerar, he said that his wife Sarah

was his sister. So, King Abimelech of Gerar had Sarah brought to him. One night God appeared to him in a dream and said, "You are going to die, because you have taken this woman; she is already married." But Abimelech had not come near her, and he said, "Lord, I am innocent! Would you destroy me and my people? Abraham himself said that she was his sister, and she said the same thing. I did this with a clear conscience, and I have done no wrong." God replied in the dream, "Yes, I know that you did it with a clear conscience; so, I kept you from sinning against me and did not let you touch her. But now, give the woman back to her husband. He is a prophet, and he will pray for you, so that you will not die. But if you do not give her back, I warn you that you are going to die, you and all your people." Early the next morning Abimelech called all his officials and told them what had happened, and they were terrified. Then Abimelech called Abraham and asked, "What have you done to us? What wrong have I done to you to make you bring this disaster on me and my kingdom? No one should ever do what you have done to me. Why did you do it?" Abraham answered, "I thought that there would be no one here who has reverence for God and that they would kill me to get my wife. She really is my sister. She is the daughter of my father, but not of my mother, and I married her. So, when God sent me from my father's house into foreign lands, I said to her, 'You can show how loyal you are to me by telling everyone that I am your brother.'" (Genesis 20:1–13 TEV)

I have had staff pastors who have violated many of the character values I am talking about and use Abraham as justification for their misconduct. Without going into a lengthy exegesis of what Abraham did, it is good to remember this happened centuries before God gave Moses the Ten Commandments. Also, there is no justifying what Abraham did because telling a lie only complicated his problems.

It does not matter who I am with, what my circumstances are, or how much it may cost me emotionally, financially, or relationally— God's principles must be consistently fleshed out in my life. God is looking for 100 percent devotion to Him. The people we minster to are powerfully impacted when they see that level of consistency in our character. Because it is so rare these days, the influence of a pastor who demonstrates this level of character will stand out like a bright light in the darkest of nights.

Lionhearted pastors understand that verbal dishonesty will destroy their reputation, their influence, and their ministry opportunities. In the hiring process I always tell our staff members that if they ever tell me a lie, shade the truth, or deceive me in any way, then our relationship will have to end because I will have no reason to be able to trust them. After serving in pastoral ministry for over four decades, the number of pastors and staff members who have violated this test of character over the years is astounding.

Many years ago, I interviewed a potential staff pastor, and after several meetings I sensed in my spirit that I should not go forward with hiring him. When I shared that with him, he called me up and pleaded with me to reconsider and asked me why I was looking elsewhere. I told him I did not think he would want to know why, but he persisted. He said that he had gotten to this place with two other churches, and the same thing happened, and he needed to understand what he was doing wrong. So foolishly I took the time to share with him my observations.

He then sent me a three-page email declaring he was dealing with those areas, thanking me for my candor, and asking me to give him another chance. (I have since learned that to override those initial instincts always results in disaster.) I allowed him and his wife to come back for another interview and hired him.

In the follow-up interview I pressed this couple to share with me the most significant crisis they had ever had in their marriage. They sat there and lied to me by saying they had had "a few problems a couple of years prior" but had gone for counseling and now were deeply committed to each other. I asked follow-up questions about whether those problems were sexual or what the nature of them was. They both said that it was "just not understanding each other," and the counseling had helped them to work on those issues. After I hired him, he shared some more information with me about a relationship he had with a previous girlfriend that had caused problems in his marriage. I asked him why he had not shared that with me during our interview. He apologized, and we moved forward, though I was convinced there was more to the story.

About a year later, his wife went to her home state to visit her family and was supposed to be gone for a week. The week turned into a month or longer, which caused me to become concerned that something else was going on. She returned and was home for a week, and he emailed me one morning and told me he was sick and would not be coming in. About an hour later, he called me and said that he needed to talk with me. He came in and told me that his wife was leaving him and going back to her home state with her family and that she had left that morning. I then asked him what was going on, and he said that in the past he had had a problem with pornography and that she did not trust him. I have dealt with many men and their wives dealing with this issue, and her reaction told me that there was more to the story. After pressing him to identify anything else that might be the issue, he assured me that was the whole problem, and nothing else was involved. There was definitely more to the story that eventually came out in one lie following another that ended the marriage.

I let him go, and on top of his lying, I discovered when we recovered his computer that he had been on a nonstop "devour Rick Addison crusade" with other staff members via email communication.

This guy had advanced degrees in ministry, had served as a staff pastor in other churches, and could not see any connection between his lying and the destruction of his marriage and ministry. I could sadly share story after story of those I have personally worked with who have the same problem and are totally shocked when their lying gets them into vocational trouble in ministry.

Guard Your Sexual Life

Lionhearted pastors also know that sexual misconduct of any kind will not only destroy their marriage but their ministry as well. Being a "one woman man" as Apostle Paul talks about in 1 Timothy 3 and Titus 1 is essential if our character is to be above reproach. At times it feels like we are living in such a sex-saturated culture that there is little distinction between the sexual misconduct of people serving in ministry and the culture itself.

Apostle Paul says in 1 Corinthians 6:18 to "flee from sexual immorality. All other sins a person commits are outside the body, but whoever sins sexually, sins against their own body."

> The body, however, is not meant for sexual immorality
> but for the Lord, and the Lord for the body. By his power
> God raised the Lord from the dead, and he will raise us

also. Do you not know that your bodies are members of Christ himself? Shall I then take the members of Christ and unite them with a prostitute? Never! Do you not know that he who unites himself with a prostitute is one with her in body? For it is said, "The two will become one flesh." But whoever is united with the Lord is one with him in spirit … Do you not know that your bodies are temples of the Holy Spirit, who is in you, whom you have received from God? You are not your own; you were bought at a price. Therefore, honor God with your bodies. (1 Corinthians 6:13–20 NIV)

To avoid sexual sin, build into your life the ethic of accountability. That means we allow someone to ask us the hard questions, and we have no hidden corners of our lives, and we do not live with "smoke and mirrors" in our lives.

The ethic of accountability started when I was a teenager. As I mentioned earlier, my dad died when he was thirty-nine years old, and I was fourteen. I am the oldest of five siblings, and during my teen years my mom leaned on and trusted me in unusual ways. Being my mom's confidante, I understood her fears and worries. After I got my driver's license, my mom did not put any restrictions on where I went and what I did. She knew she did not have to because if I told her I was with a particular friend, she knew that this was who I was with and that if anyone else joined us, I would let her know. That was before there were even beepers and certainly not cell phones, and if anything changed about the people, places, and things with which I was engaged, I would call her from a payphone and let her know what was going on. I did not want to add to the challenges of her life by her worrying about me, and I intuitively knew that kind of accountability was not only good for her, but it was good for me as well.

When Karon and I got married, I have continued that same practice with her for over four decades now. There is no greater deterrent to moral failure than total accountability. Either my wife knows where I am all day every day or my assistant does during the ministry workday. Everyone I know who messes up sexually has lots of unaccounted-for time in their lives. I have long said that the greatest tool Satan has in his bag of sexual tricks for the average man is anonymity and unaccounted-for time.

In twenty months, I had three staff members released because of their practice of homosexuality. Two of them were in leading ministry positions in our church. The reactions of all three were remarkably different from each other. The first was immediately honest about what he was involved in and deeply repentant. The second was not in a lead ministry position, and he just disappeared. The third attempted to lie his way out. When that did not work, he then began an eighteen-month assault on me and the church.

Only God Himself knows the extent of the amount of damage those people have done to our church and to the people we serve.

It has always been hard for me to understand that if you have the moral values of an alley cat why you choose to serve in ministry when what you are doing will ultimately be found out.

The adage "an ounce of prevention is worth a pound of cure" certainly applies to managing the moral aspects of our character.

When I was a small boy and just beginning to understand sexuality, I decided I was not going to have sex until I got married. Unbeknownst to me, my future wife made the same decision. One of the greatest gifts we have given to each other was our virginity. When we got married in

August 1974, we made a commitment that we would build practices in our lives that would help facilitate sexual faithfulness in our marriage. These are the precepts we agreed to:

- We would not be in a room alone with someone of the opposite sex with the door closed.
- We would not be in a vehicle alone with someone of the opposite sex.
- We would not meet someone of the opposite sex alone for a meal, coffee, or in any other setting that could be conducive to something inappropriate developing.
- We would be fully accountable to each other for where we were and who we were with all day, every day.

I have said to our staff many times that "two is company and three is security." When it is just two of you, it is easy for some form of emotional intimacy to develop, which will never happen if there are three of you. Also, when you are alone with someone of the opposite sex, you put yourself in an indefensible position where it is just your word against their word. Too much risk is involved to violate those principles. By God's grace and mercy, Karon and I have been sexually faithful to each other since we exchanged our marriage vows on August 23, 1974.

When we are tempted sexually it is always helpful to think about the devastating effect our selfishness will have on the people we love in our lives. When I am tempted sexually, I focus on how such a sin will devastate the most loyal person in my life, my wife, Karon. It would have a tragic effect on our sons, our grandchildren, and extended family members. It would be spiritually destructive to those I have preached to for decades who have trusted and believed in me. It would shake our church organizationally and could even destroy it. On top of all of that, everyone who sins sexually simultaneously becomes a prolific liar, cheat, and untrustworthy person. It makes people become full of self-loathing, and they even lose respect for themselves.

Lionhearted pastors know that when they lose their sexual integrity, they have really lost everything. Effective ministry requires authenticity, honesty, and moral integrity. Without these, I have nothing convincing to teach to someone else. I have lost the right to be heard and respected. That is why managing yourself is a matter of managing your character.

CHAPTER 7

First Fruits

God repeatedly tells us He must be first in every aspect of our lives. Honoring God with our money always starts by living by the biblical principle of "first." What that means is God wants to be first in everything in our lives, including our money. Going clear back to the dawn of creation, when Cain and Abel gave God their offerings, God accepted Abel's because he gave God "the first born of his flocks." Cain's sacrifice was rejected because he gave God "of the fruit of his fields." God does not want to receive the leftovers of our resources; he wants to be first.

> Abel kept flocks, and Cain worked the soil. In the course of time Cain brought some of the fruits of the soil as an offering to the LORD. And Abel also brought an offering—fat portions from some of the firstborn of his flock. The LORD looked with favor on Abel and his offering, but on Cain and his offering he did not look with favor. So, Cain was very angry, and his face was downcast. Then the LORD said to Cain, "Why are you angry? Why is your face downcast? If you do what is right, will you not be accepted? But if you do

not do what is right, sin is crouching at your door; it desires to have you, but you must rule over it." (Genesis 4:2–7 NIV)

The very first commandment, "You shall have no other God before me" (Exodus 20:3 NIV) is most evident in where God is in the financial affairs of our lives. Spiritual integrity requires I make God "first" in all my resources. God wants the first part of our time, the first part of our talents and abilities, and the first part of our finances. Over the years I have discovered many staff members have no comprehension of what the Bible says about "the principle of first" in both the Old Testament and the New Testament. For more insights into what God says about this I recommend the book *The Blessed Life*, by Robert Morris. I believe his insights are so profound that when someone makes their first recorded contribution, we mail them that book.

Because we have discovered that so many staff members struggle to "return the tithe to God" through giving to the church, we have had to include a commitment to tithing as a part of our employment agreement when we hire staff members. All of them will sign it, but because of the problem of "situational ethics" I described earlier, if they are going through a financial challenge, they just stop returning what belongs to God and never say anything about it until it is challenged.

Some of their responses are totally unbelievable. This is a common excuse: "I changed my checking account to a different bank, and it was set up to come out automatically." Or, "You mean they have not been sending a check to the church?" If it was believable, then it tells me that they probably have an issue with financial mismanagement, which concerns me as much as not returning the tithe to God. That leaves me wondering how many of their bills are not being paid as well and what else they are being sloppy about in their personal lives.

Karon and I long ago quit tithing and practice what we call "generous giving." That simply means that we have decided we will never spend more money on a house, a car, or anything else than we return to God through our giving. For many years we have returned to God much more than a tithe. Up to this point the only thing the IRS has ever audited me for is the amount of our contributions. When I sent in the canceled checks, their response was "no additional taxes required!" When I stand before God Almighty one day, and He is doing the audit of my life, I want Him to say of how we have handled the financial blessings in our lives, "Rick Addison, I see that you have had no other God before me … well done good and faithful servant."

A reputation for sloppiness in our personal financial affairs is a horrible testimony for a pastor to have in a community. It not only affects their personal world, but it also has a lot of impact on their "ministry life" as well. All these sinful ways— not telling the truth, sexual misconduct, and poor financial stewardship—are frequently interwoven into a person's life and will ultimately shipwreck his or her ministry opportunities and effectiveness.

Don't Be a Sower of Discord and Division

Apostle Paul says if we are a part of division and discord, we are serving our own ambitions. Pay close attention to these verses in Romans 16:17–19 (ESV):

> I urge you, brothers, to *watch out for those who cause divisions* and put obstacles in your way that are contrary to the teaching you have learned. Keep away from them. For *such people are not serving the Lord Jesus Christ, but their own appetites.* By smooth talk and flattery, they

deceive the minds of naïve people. Everyone has heard about your obedience, so I am full of joy over you; but I want you to be wise about what is good, and innocent about what is evil (emphasis mine).

We have experienced having ministry staff members who, because they are serving their own self-centered plans, will hire away a group of people and go start a church in our community. It is all because they are serving their own ambitions. Apostle Paul says that these people are not serving the Lord Jesus Christ but their own appetites, and they deceive the minds of naïve people. I never want to be classified as being someone who sows division and discord. God has helped us over the course of our four decades of ministry to be a force for unity and harmony. If we focus on what is right for the church, then we will transform how we deal with our own personal ambitions.

I have a difficult time understanding where people who are serving in vocational ministry think they can divide the body of Christ and at the same time grow the church of Jesus Christ. When I accepted a call to serve as a pastor, one of my first commitments to God was that I would never be a part of dividing his body.

Do Not Build on Another Man's Foundation

In Romans 15:20 (NIV) Apostle Paul says, "It has always been my ambition to preach the gospel where Christ was not known, so that I would not be building on someone else's foundation." I see that principle repeatedly violated.

I had a former staff member who violated this principle; he had left our church and was gone for a little over a year and then returned and started a new church in our community and targeted hundreds of people in our congregation. Through a series of events, things weren't working out so well for him, and he wanted to have a meeting.

"You know, Rick," he said, "I know that things are not right between us, and I would like for them to be. But I don't know where to start."

I said, *"Well, I do,"* and shared with him that what he had done was come to our town to start his church not because we did not have enough churches but because he knew he would have a ready audience. I told him if I went back to any of the previous four churches I had pastored, even though it had been many years, or even decades, since I had been there, and I started a church in one of those communities, I would go knowing that within a year, about half of the people I used to pastor (if they were still alive) would be worshipping with me in the next year.

"You knew what you were doing when you came here," I told him calmly, then I shared with him what Apostle Paul said about not building on someone else's foundation and how important it is that we do not build our ministry on another man's ministry.

In the church today, we have a tremendous amount of what I call "guppy swapping." We believe that if we take guppies out of one church's aquarium and put them in our aquarium, the church will be growing when really the church is not growing at all. I explained to this young man it looks like you could take guppies out of our aquarium and put them in yours and that would be something that would result in your ministry growing and our ministry diminishing. I explained to him that if you go to the guppy shop and buy guppies, and you take that little guppy out of the aquarium it was born in and has lived its entire life in, and you put it in a little plastic bag and take it home and put it in your aquarium, there is a mortality rate of somewhere around 25 percent. That's why the guppy shop always says that if your guppy dies in the next forty-eight hours, they'll give you another one.

"Unfortunately, we are not dealing with guppies here," I told him. "Let us say the mortality rate is not 25 percent. Let's say it's 5 percent. When you swap three hundred people from The Grace Place's "aquarium" and put them in your "aquarium," even if there is just a 5 percent spiritual mortality rate, then understand that you created spiritual confusion in the lives of many people by doing what you did, not only in their lives but in the lives of people in their families and in their circle of friends. Jesus says that is a serious offense—and that by causing that confusion, it would be better if a millstone was hung around your neck, and you were thrown into the depths of the sea.

I still think most of us understand that building on another man's ministry is something that violates all kinds of principles. Apostle Paul talks about that in 2 Corinthians 10:16 (New English Translation) where he says, "so that we may preach the gospel in the regions that lie beyond you, and not boast of work already done in another person's area." He goes on to say, "we'll be able to preach the good news to other cities that are far beyond you where no one else is working."

Behind every violation of ministry ethics is the sin of coveting. When God gave Moses the Ten Commandments, He started off by saying, "You shall have no other gods before me." Then He ended the Ten Commandments with the tenth one stating we "should not covet our neighbor's house, nor his wife, his male servant, his female servant, his ox, his donkey, or anything that belongs to his neighbor." Many times, the problem behind division and discord is really wanting what somebody else has. For example, if you are a staff member, you want to become the senior pastor. If you are the senior pastor, you want to become the pastor of a larger church within the organization of which you're a part. If you are in a denomination, you may be coveting some leadership role in that denomination. Whenever you allow yourself to succumb to the sin of coveting, it opens the door for all kinds of other issues in our lives that create discord and disharmony.

Shepherds Vs. Hirelings

There are three kinds of people who seek to serve in ministry: the wise, the foolish and the evil. Wise spiritual leaders are "shepherds," those who really care for the flock, who see what they do as a ministry or as a calling from God and not a job. "Fools and evil people" are those we would describe as "hirelings." Those are the people who do not really care about the flock and the sheep; as Apostle Paul says, they are not really in "ministry" to "serve our Lord Jesus Christ … but such people are … serving … their own appetites (their own personal ambitions)" (Romans 16:18 NIV).

Jesus tells us that the shepherd cares for the sheep and that the hireling runs away. The hired hand, He says in John 10:12–13 (NIV), is not the shepherd who owns the sheep. When he sees a wolf coming, he abandons the sheep and runs away. Then the wolf attacks the flock and scatters it. The man runs away because he is a hired hand and cares nothing for the sheep. Many people want a ministry title but treat it like it is a job. They do not see themselves as shepherds. I know they are because any time something happens that they don't like, they are ready to quit, and many times do quit. These same people will create as much chaos as is possible when they do and destroy as many of the flock as they can destroy. It creates havoc in the church and confusion.

If you are a true shepherd, it does not matter whether you are the senior pastor, a staff pastor, or what other responsibilities you may have, a shepherd does not run away. A shepherd cares for the sheep and would never do anything destructive to that flock. When we left the previous four churches we pastored, I did everything I could to leave the church in better shape than I had found it. Because of that, when Karon and I completed thirty years of ministry, we had what we called a "reunion tour." We went back to the four churches we had pastored prior to coming to The Grace Place. We had meetings with people in those churches. We were warmly welcomed because we did not divide or polarize those churches when we transitioned.

I think of all the people I know in ministry, and very few of them can return to those previous places of ministry and be welcomed. The primary reason is because they functioned like hirelings and were destructive to the flock whenever they left those ministries.

How you finish your ministry with a church will determine how you and your ministry are remembered. If you finish well, you are remembered with fondness. If you finish poorly, anything positive you ever did in ministry will not even be remembered because all people will remember is how poorly you finished!

Lionhearted leaders build into their lives some real principles that keep them on the right path. I challenge us all not to be blown around by every wind of doctrine. Understand that when we do violate these principles, it has a lot of negative effect on other people. God has a terrific opportunity for all of us to serve Him. There are incredible needs everywhere. There are people all around us who do not know Jesus Christ. There is way too much to do in advancing the kingdom to "play church." Lionhearted pastors see the Church (with a big "C") and it changes the way they do ministry. They do not just focus on what is going to advance their organization. They do ministry focusing on what is going to advance the kingdom of Jesus Christ.

I encourage all of us to understand how essential it is that we use the influence God has given us to make an unbelievable impact for the kingdom of Jesus Christ. If you will apply these principles to your life and the way you do ministry, it will profoundly affect the long-term impact of your ministry and the church will truly prevail against the very gates of hell!

CHAPTER 8

Foundations Are Important

If you are buying or building a home, there is a part of the house you do not easily see, but it is what everything else stands on—the foundation. Over the years I have seen people try to build a ministry without laying the right foundations, and it always produces a disaster.

If you don't start building a church by laying the right foundation, you will discover it will eventually implode. I am going to share biblical principles about how the church should be structured if the pastor is to lead the church for the long haul.

When you analyze declining churches or those that go through a repeated series of growth and decline, generally some foundational issues need to be changed. I have repeatedly talked to pastors and leaders in those churches who tell me they have tried everything, but nothing ever seems to work in a sustained way.

It is obvious that trying one more church growth gimmick is not going to solve a leadership problem, a spiritual problem, an organizational problem, a philosophical problem, or the problem of having either no strategies or the wrong strategies. A pastor may be a tremendous leader and a real man of God. If he is dealing with church structures that tie his leadership hands, then the only development the church will experience is what the pastor can do relationally. If a church has great organizational structures and the right philosophy but has a spiritually shallow leader, the church will never realize its potential.

During the interview process, I did enough research on The Grace Place to know there were some changes to the church structures that had to take place for the church to be able to move forward. The church had what was called an "open board," where any man who claimed to be a Christ follower, attended regularly, and contributed financially could come to any meeting, make a motion on any matter, and then could walk away without any sense of ongoing responsibility.

Shortly before I came, they had one of their meetings and a motion was made by someone who wanted to purchase a big diesel-powered mower. This man brought some other friends with him to the meeting to vote with him, and the motion passed. They wiped out the financial resources to buy this mower, which wasn't even needed, and didn't return for any subsequent meetings.

During the interview we also discussed the shortcomings of their church structures. I explained the value of an actual congregation elder led system of church government and how important it was to build it on the right foundation. Looking back on it, that is one of the primary reasons we have been able to lead this church for so long.

I am always surprised at how little research many pastors do into the structures of a church before they arrive for an interview. In fact, I have had numerous conversations with pastors who are dealing with nonbiblical church structures that are causing all kinds of challenges, conflicts, and short-term ministries. When I ask them why they didn't address those issues before they accepted an invitation to become the pastor of that church, they will say things like: "I thought I could change it after I got there," or "I must have wanted to make a transition so badly that all I saw was the potential and not the problems."

When we went to our first church, I was young and naïve and did not have a clue as to how important church structures were, nor how the history of the church was a predictor of what was to come. After our experience with the tractor guy, I became wiser and began to do a lot more research focused on analyzing the potential problem people and structures. By the time we made this last transition, I had learned to not only identify future problem people but organizational problems as well.

In fact, one of the churches that contacted us during our transition time seemed to be an attractive opportunity for us to expand and grow. They had a beautiful building located in a fantastic location in the city. During my preinterview research I discovered the guy who donated the property to the church had set it up where he and his son were the only trustees—and they were lifetime trustees as well. The donor told me that it was set up that way because they did not want to lose control of "their assets." I explained to him that if they gave the property to the church, it was really "giving" it to God, which meant it wouldn't be "their asset" any longer. During the interview I questioned their reasoning and described my concerns and ultimately told them they would have to change this setup before I would accept an invitation to come check it out. They refused to make those changes, so I declined the ministry opportunity. My concerns proved to be correct, and that church went through a time of "troubled waters" and today no longer exists. It was not long until the church split due to what I call powerbroker church members. I have thanked God repeatedly for saving us from that inevitable heartbreak.

Biblical Church Structures

I grew up in a small church environment where most pastors focused on making everyone happy. Many smaller churches are structured to keep a pastor from leading effectively, since this is an impossible task.

For example, because of congregational rule structures, many of those churches empower a local member to gain tremendous influence and power. We called them "church bosses."

Lionhearted pastors have learned to lead with tremendous God-confidence and to not be intimidated by those people. If a church is led by a strong pastor and elder-led council, it will likely result in an inevitable backlash from people who feel like they are losing their power. These backlashes will frequently catch a leader by surprise but are not insurmountable.

The Bible Calls the Church a Body

"For just as each of us has one body with many members, and these members do not all have the same function, so in Christ we, though many, form one body, and each member belongs to all the others" (Romans 12:4–5 NIV).

The body is made up of many parts. The head is where the directions for the body come from. The skeleton gives the body structure. The internal organs keep the body alive. The external parts of the body are what everyone sees and associates with the functions of the body.

The Lead Pastor Is the Head

God calls lead pastors to be the *indisputable leader of the church*. Most of us understand that a two-headed animal only ends up in the zoo or in a circus. The Bible teaches us there can only be one person as the human head of a church. (We know the Bible teaches that Jesus is the spiritual head of the church.) Having the pastor as the head of the church runs counter to the way a lot of churches are structured. God has always led His people through God-appointed, God-directed leaders. Every church I know that flounders does so due to a debate over who is the true leader.

Because God calls the head pastor to lead the church, he must be prepared to lead organizationally. I know a lot of guys do not think they are particularly good at that, so they don't deal with those responsibilities very well. In all fairness, I would just say that many existing church structures make leading extremely difficult for the head pastor.

A pastor who is in a dysfunctional church will spend most of their time keeping everybody happy and in agreement. Because of that they waste most of their leadership energy on just trying to lead the already convinced. This unfortunately ties the hands of the pastor, and as a result his best leadership energy does not go into ministry strategies, and he cannot focus on connecting the church in a more constructive way to the needs of people in their community. That can waste an immense amount of leadership energy.

I remember when Karon and I first came to Community Bible Chapel, which later became The Grace Place, a large dated wooden podium was used for preaching. It was built by a church member who was "married" to the idea that the pastor would preach from it. It became a source of pride for that member, and I knew if I preached behind it, then I would be giving a lot of focus to the wrong things and not lead with openness. This became a source of contention with everyone worrying about what this member thought instead of the calling of the church.

Lionhearted pastors are spiritually equipped to deal with the *negative stresses* of leading the church. I am careful about not letting our congregational elders take the organizational negatives on the chin. Because they do not have the same calling that I do, they are not equipped emotionally to deal with those stresses and backlash. They don't keep me awake at night, but they will cause others to lose sleep because they are not called to do what we are called to do. If you are a lead pastor or a senior pastor, understand that God will give you the strength you need to deal with those situational matters such as staffing and financial responsibilities.

A lionhearted pastor will have a *vision* for the church's next steps in ministry development. We have had some amazing miracles take place at The Grace Place. Let me tell you a little story about one. It all started following a clear God call I had in the middle of the night following an exhaustive prayer time. After praying until I had no more words to say, I sat my chair in our den and asked God to speak to me. After sitting there for a while listening to God, I sensed the Holy Spirit telling me to have our bookkeeper handwrite new payoff checks each month when we made the mortgage payments. At the end of each of our staff meetings we would lay our hands on the envelop holding those checks and pray a prayer of faith that God would deliver us from the slavery of debt.

About six months after we started those prayers, I read Mark Batterson's book *The Circle Maker*. The message of the book reinforced and verified that what we were doing was on track, but we also started a couple of other prayer circles, and as a result we are seeing the most amazing things happen I have ever experienced in over four decades of pastoral ministry.

A few years after we started the financial freedom prayer circle, we experienced a miracle unlike anything we had ever seen before. I woke up on that day at 5:00 a.m., and my wife felt me stirring around in the bed.

"What is going on?" she asked.

I said, "God just spoke to me and told me today was going to be a day of miracles!"

I can tell you the exact day, December 20, 2016. That day I had lunch with one of our businessmen who handed me an envelope and told me to give it to the bookkeeper. It was a check for $60,000.

When I told my wife over dinner that evening, she asked, "Rick is that the miracle?"

Well, it was a miracle, but not *the* miracle! That afternoon at four thirty, one of the businessmen in our church walked into my office. He had one of our regular contribution envelopes in his hand that we use every weekend. Inside was a personal tithe check for $3.4 million! God is in the business of answering prayers! Lionhearted pastors and leaders will experience blessings from God that we would otherwise miss by short-term leadership. We suddenly went from $4 million of debt to zero debt in less than two years.

The Overseers Are the Internal Organs

In our church structure we have four selected overseers, and they are all pastors of their own churches. All of them have been serving in senior leadership for twenty years or longer. Their churches are far enough away from The Grace Place so that no decision they ever make could have any kind of impact on their own ministries. I describe the overseers as the *internal organs* of the church, an incredibly important part.

My dad was killed by a drunk driver in 1969. He had been a pastor of his church in Findlay, Ohio, for nine years at the time he was killed. He was just thirty-nine years old. I watched that church go through the most amazing struggles after Dad was killed. They went through two or three pastors.

When Karon and I left the church, we were pastoring in Michigan but went back so I could serve as the pastor of my dad's church. It was twelve years after Dad was killed. It took us going there for that church to find its equilibrium. The unfortunate reality is that people left the church, and it struggled for about a decade because it did not have an overseer-type structure to hold it steady during the shock of my dad's death.

We have a church in our community where the senior pastor died unexpectedly several years ago, and I have watched that church go through a lot of amazing challenges, and the succeeding pastor has not led it well. I believe a lot of their problems would have been avoided if they had developed overseer structure.

The overseers of the church hold me accountable for my spiritual life—my biblical, moral, ethical, and marital faithfulness. They are the only group who can remove me from leading the church. If the congregational elders are aware there is a deficit in some area, they then will have the overseers investigate it and deal with it. If you have watched a church go through the process of having to remove the pastor, you know that this almost always creates incredible internal polarization. The overseers are much better equipped spiritually and through their calling to deal with those kinds of challenges.

They also direct the selection of a new pastor when a vacancy occurs. If I were to drop dead or resign, the overseers are the ones who go through the process of selecting a replacement pastor. They would then recommend who they selected to the congregational elders for approval. The amount of experience of the overseers in place will reduce the internal politicking that goes on with staff members when there is a vacancy.

The Congregational Elders Are the Skeletal Structure

Our congregational elders serve the church body as the skeletal structure of the church. A lot of churches put their elders on public display all the time. At The Grace Place, most of the people have no idea who most of the elders are.

The human body has many bones. If all the bones are where they are supposed to be, they are not visible other than the arm or leg, for example, which have shape and function because of the skeletal structure. If you saw the bone, you would look at it and say, "Rick, you just seriously injured yourself, and you need to get to the hospital and get that fixed quickly because it's a compound fracture."

But the skeletal structure of the body is extremely important. My mother had Parkinson's disease before she died, and I watched as the ravages of that disease literally destroyed her body's ability to function. If you do not think the skeletal structure is important, you certainly recognize its importance whenever disease takes its function away. That is why I think the function of the congregational elders as skeletal is so important.

We require all congregational elders to give clear testimony of having a life-changing and personal relationship with Jesus Christ. I remember talking to a pastor several years ago who told me that one of his elders was creating all kinds of problems for him. He had eventually asked this man if he had ever experienced a life-changing relationship through faith in Jesus Christ as his savior. The man acknowledged he had never experienced that. My obvious next question was to ask if they had removed him from leadership. He told me they had not. I remember hanging up my phone and saying to myself, *That guy is not a lionhearted leader.* He was too timid to take the next obvious step.

All congregational elders are responsible to model a godly lifestyle. I always remind our elders that to "go up, they must give up" rights in exchange for responsibilities. That simply means the more influence a person has, the fewer rights they have.

Almost all our congregational elders are involved in one of our weekly prayer circle meetings. They understand they are to defend and protect the integrity of the church in the community.

In the nearly three decades I have been at The Grace Place, we have had to remove an elder on just two occasions for not fulfilling their responsibilities. Each time it was because an ambitious and divisive staff member got on the inside with an elder and attempted a coup. Since we developed the overseer structure, that has not happened because removal of the senior pastor must be done by the overseer. Over and over, I have seen how God has used this organization to help the church maintain stability in potentially negative situations.

The Deacons and Deaconesses Are the Visible Parts of the Body (arms, legs, hands, feet, etc.)

We do not use the word *deacon* or *deaconess* as a title because it is used by so many churches in so many ways. The function of a deacon in a Catholic church, in a Methodist church, in a Lutheran church, and in a Baptist church is so different. Because of the confusion, we just focus on the role.

But deacons and deaconesses are leaders of various ministries and are highly visible in our church. Our Celebrate Recovery director, Stephanie Johnston, is one of the most amazing leaders I know and is doing an incredible job with this ministry. Elders, on the other hand, are not highly visible. But her ministry, because it is a visible part of the body, is highly visible.

Our deacons and deaconesses are ministry staff or volunteers who serve as ministry leaders of various departments like men's, communion, and prayer ministries. Their role is to serve as the ministry hands and feet of the church. This team oversees the day-to-day ministry and operations of the church. These staff pastors, ministry directors, and lay leaders serve the congregation and are responsible for the development of the spiritual life of the church.

Practical Ways to Implement Structural Changes in Your Church

To successfully implement structural change, you must *know what you believe* the Bible teaches about church structure.

Do not just believe what I say about it. Study your Bible. Come to an understanding where you are convinced in your own heart that this is how the church of Jesus Christ ought to be structured. When you get to that point, you can lead with amazing confidence. When you know this is exactly how the church should be structured, it will give you great boldness.

Please do not change for the sake of change. Evaluate what needs to be changed. Take stock and do an inventory first, then choose your battles. I know some pastors who seem to just be searching for the next fight. I usually don't have to go looking for one. I think it just happens when I put my shoes on in the morning.

I had a pastor friend. He and I were about the same age and were great friends for over thirty years. I was talking to him one day, and he told me about pushing the church he served to make a change that was best in his opinion. I thought his recommendation was ridiculous.

"What in the world are you pushing this for?" I asked incredulously. "Does it make a bit of difference organizationally?"

He said, "No."

I asked, "Does it make a bit of difference in what you're going to preach next weekend?"

He said, "No."

I then said, "Well, why in the world are you trying to change something that is only causing conflict?" He didn't have an answer. In less than a year the church had a huge split, and he left the church not too long afterward, and I believe this contributed to his early decline in health and early death in his fifties.

I always try to choose my battles. There are things I will die for, and there are things that I will not waste a headache over. So do not make changes just for the sake of change.

Make structural changes that are in the long-term good of the church, not to benefit yourself. Every change we have made I have looked at and asked, "Is this is for the long-term benefit of The Grace Place?" I will be the pastor of the church for only a certain period. We want to make adjustments that are done for the church's long-term benefit.

Making structural changes requires courageously challenging insubordinate people. Jesus would describe an insubordinate person as somebody who is a tare sown among the wheat or as a wolf who disguises himself by putting on sheep's clothing. If you do not think they are in the church, then wake up because Satan has his agents in every church.

One of the biggest mistakes I have ever made in ministry is trying to treat a wolf who wears a sheep's disguise like a wayward sheep. You know a wolf is a wolf because wolves divide and devour.

It takes courage to challenge an insubordinate person, but it's important not to give them time to do their work, because all they will do is destroy. I am not talking about confronting them the first day you meet them, but be alert to who they are when you see their behaviors.

If I have made one mistake in ministry that I could undo, it would be that I have let wolves disguised in sheep's costume stay way too long. I have discovered something else about disguised wolves—we have been giving some of them a paycheck they didn't deserve. They are staff members I knew I should have fired but was reluctant to do so. If you have somebody on your staff right now that you know you need to let go, then take care of business. Please use wisdom in doing it, but go do it.

As it states in Matthew 7:15 (NIV): "Watch out for false prophets. They come to you in sheep's clothing, but inwardly they are ferocious wolves."

Use existing structures to systematically make changes through your existing leadership body. Do not begin the process of structural changes unless you are committed to the church. I have talked to many pastors who begin the process of change, and when they run into what looks like a roadblock, they leave the church and move somewhere else.

When we came to The Grace Place, I made a "best years of my life" personal commitment to this church. That simply means that through the best of times or the worst of times I am committed to being here and seeing the church through whatever we are dealing with. That level of commitment creates trust and steady leadership that makes substantial change possible.

Even though that is my attitude, I never got up in the first few years of our leadership and made public declarations of my commitment. People sensed it without me saying it. One of my predecessors at a previous church I served had declared publicly many times he was there for life, and five years later he left the church. That caused a huge amount of confusion for the people in the church and a lot of unnecessary challenges for me. It was only after I had been at The Grace Place about fifteen years that I started declaring "one of the reasons I was born was to serve this church." By then my commitment and dedication to the church had become obvious to most parishioners.

Lionhearted pastors and leaders who are committed for the long haul should be patient with the process. I was wrapping up my graduate program when we went to Stuart. I had a conversation with my graduate thesis project adviser. I was contemplating rewriting the bylaws of the church as a part of the project. He gave me some good advice, particularly coming from academia (with which I am typically not overly impressed). He said, "Rick, you have a really unique opportunity with this church that not many pastors have." He was aware that I had already rearranged some of the church's organizational structures during the negotiating process of my coming to serve as their pastor. He said, "What I would suggest is that you implement your structural changes through the existing board that you have in place one piece at a time until you have adjusted the structure to what you believe it ought to be. Once it has been adjusted, *then* write your bylaws to reflect what is already in place."

That is what we have done. We have radically changed the structure of the church without division, and it is because we did it one piece at a time. I was at The Grace Place for twenty-three years before we finally rewrote the bylaws to reflect who we have become.

The Benefits of Biblical Church Structures

Biblical church structures facilitate the growth and development of the church. When the leaders of the church understand that one of their primary responsibilities is to envision a preferred future for the church and anticipate the church's next steps, growth is almost inevitable. Ungodly church structures are a breeding ground for conflict, power-grabs, and manipulation that is exhausting, discouraging, and defeating to the lead pastor.

Biblical church structures remove the leash of unending committee meetings. Too many pastors expend most of their leadership energy on getting all their various committees to agree. These structures also enable the lead pastor to really lead with vision, purpose, and clarity.

In addition, biblical church structures give the church stability during what I call a "ministry hurricane" used by Satan to challenge every aspect of the ministries of your church. Just like a house that is built to withstand the forces of a hurricane and suffer only minimal damage, biblical church structures are designed by God to do the same thing for the church organizationally.

If you are anywhere long enough, you are going to go through a ministry "hurricane."

I was talking with a leader of an organization that equipped leaders around the world and shared with him some challenges with which we were dealing involving a former staff pastor. He responded that "anytime you are committed to a church for the long haul, somewhere between years eighteen and twenty, they are going to go through a Waterloo-type experience." Basically expect problem areas to come up.

The structures of the church are best seen as being sound when you are going through a storm. It is then that you know whether the ship of ministry holds together or falls apart. That is another reason why the right kinds of church structures are so important.

Biblical church structures protect the church from fraudulent leaders and are designed by God to help a church keep its focus even when there is a change in pastoral leadership. They even protect the church from a pastor who is a wolf, disguised as a sheep.

The Grace Place is a nondenominational church. As a result, we are acutely aware that a fraudulent leader could come in and literally run everybody else off. Then this pastor and his wife could end up the only trustees left and could sell millions of dollars of church property.

I read of a pastor who was arrested several years ago for inappropriate sexual behavior. His story was on the news, and as a result the church he pastored collapsed. That left him and his wife as the two remaining trustees. When the property was sold, the check was written to this man and his wife. That is an extreme example of what a fraudulent leader can do, but our structures make it impossible for anyone to sell the property without the approval of the overseers.

It is important to always remember that God wants to do something incredibly powerful with your ministry to advance His kingdom through your church.

We understand that foundations are incredibly important in buildings; they are even more important in ministries. Foundation building is hard work; it does not look beautiful but is essential if you are going to build a ministry that will last. Let me encourage you to understand that without the right foundations, your ministry will never make it for the long haul.

All of us have seen ministry after ministry collapse because the leader did not build the right stuff into the foundations. God wants your ministry to last and have profound influence on the lives of people long after you are gone.

CHAPTER 9

Vision

Many years ago, a friend and I visited a church in another state to meet with the senior pastor. When we drove onto the campus, all the church facilities were incredible. Along with these beautiful church buildings they had an assisted living facility, Christian school, and other ministry structures. I turned to my friend and said, "This is the product of someone who had a huge vision."

From what I understand, around 95 percent of all the people in America do not have any written goals for their lives. The problem is that most people do not have problems reaching goals; they have a problem with setting goals. I have discovered that once you establish goals, it's much easier to reach them.

Vision or Daydreaming?

When I was in a literature class in high school, I read a story about a man named Walter Mitty. He is a real dreamer. He takes his wife to the doctor, and he dreams that he is a submarine captain. He takes her to the beauty parlor and dreams that he is a world-renowned surgeon. He dreams on and on and right in the middle of his dream his wife interrupts him to bring him back to the reality of his nightmare in life. When we talk about vision and dreams, we are not talking about daydreaming and Walter Mitty types of dreams. Those dreams are escapes not direction for our lives and leadership.

In Proverbs 16:3 (MSG), Solomon says: "Put GOD in charge of your work, then what you have planned will take place."

A God-Given Dream

In the Old Testament there is the story of man who accomplished great things for God despite huge setbacks, betrayals, and injustice. His story is found in Genesis 37:5–11 (MSG).

> Joseph had a dream. When he told it to his brothers, they hated him even more. He said, "Listen to this dream I had. We were all out in the field gathering bundles of wheat. All of a sudden my bundle stood straight up and your bundles circled around it and bowed down to mine." His brothers said, "So! You're going to rule us? You're going to boss us around?" And they hated him more than ever because of his dreams and the way he talked. He had another dream and told this one also to his brothers: "I dreamed another dream—the sun and moon and eleven stars bowed down to me!" When he told it to his father and brothers, his father reprimanded him: "What's with all this dreaming? Am I and your mother and your brothers all supposed to bow down to you?" Now his brothers were really jealous; but his father brooded over the whole business.

Joseph's brothers got so angry with him they were going to kill him but instead decided to sell him to some slave traders who took Joseph down to Egypt. There he was bought by a man named Potiphar who eventually put Joseph in charge of running his household. Potiphar's wife wanted to have an affair with Joseph, and he kept eluding her until one day she caught him alone. When he turned down her advances, she grabbed his coat and told her husband Joseph tried to rape her. He then went to prison and was there for a long time, Finally the king of Egypt had a dream no one could interpret. Since Joseph was good at interpreting dreams, the king sent for him, and he accurately interpreted the dream and told the king there was going to be seven years of abundance and seven years of famine (Genesis 41:25–41 New King James Version):

> Then Joseph said to Pharaoh, "The dreams of Pharaoh are one; God has shown Pharaoh what He is about to do: The seven good cows are seven years, and the seven good heads are seven years; the dreams are one. And the seven thin and ugly cows which came up after them are seven years, and the seven empty heads blighted by the east wind are seven years of famine. This is the thing which I have spoken to Pharaoh. God has shown Pharaoh what He is about to do. Indeed, seven years of great plenty will come throughout all the land of Egypt; but after them seven years of famine will arise, and all the plenty will be forgotten in the land of Egypt; and the famine will deplete the land. So, the plenty will not be known in the land because of the famine following, for it will be very severe. And the dream was repeated to

Pharaoh twice because the thing is established by God, and God will shortly bring it to pass.

Now therefore, let Pharaoh select a discerning and wise man, and set him over the land of Egypt. Let Pharaoh do this, and let him appoint officers over the land, to collect one-fifth of the produce of the land of Egypt in the seven plentiful years. And let them gather all the food of those good years that are coming, and store up grain under the authority of Pharaoh, and let them keep food in the cities. Then that food shall be as a reserve for the land for the seven years of famine which shall be in the land of Egypt, that the land may not perish during the famine." So the advice was good in the eyes of Pharaoh and in the eyes of all his servants.

And Pharaoh said to his servants, "Can we find such a one as this, a man in whom is the Spirit of God?" Then Pharaoh said to Joseph, "Inasmuch as God has shown you all this, there is no one as discerning and wise as you. You shall be over my house, and all my people shall be ruled according to your word; only in regard to the throne will I be greater than you." And Pharaoh said to Joseph, "See, I have set you over all the land of Egypt."

Joseph was able to move forward with the right attitude despite being hated by his brothers, falsely accused by Potiphar's wife, and being forgotten in prison because he had this compelling vision of what God wanted to do with his life. He knew in the darkest of times that God was not through with him, that he would one day see what he had envisioned many years earlier.

After becoming second in command of Egypt, the nation goes through the seven years of plenty, then the seven years of famine began, and after a few years what Joseph envisioned happening came to pass:

> Now Joseph was governor over the land; and it was he who sold to all the people of the land. And Joseph's brothers came and bowed down before him with their faces to the earth. Joseph saw his brothers and recognized them, but he acted as a stranger to them and spoke roughly to them. Then he said to them, "Where do you come from?" And they said, "From the land of Canaan to buy food." So Joseph recognized his brothers, but they did not recognize him. Then Joseph remembered the dreams which he had dreamed about them. (Genesis 42:6–9 NKJV)

> Vision is a powerful tool God uses to keep us on track and focused on what He wants to do through our lives and ministry.

For the year prior to engaging with Stuart, my wife and I had prayed together each day, and both of us were individually fasting and praying for God to give us clear direction for our next steps in ministry.

My mother lived about twelve miles from The Grace Place. We were visiting her over our Christmas break, and I was going to town one day when I had a vision of a multitude of people coming through our doors. I know exactly where I was when I had a brief but clear vision I now know was from God (this was not something I was seeking, nor something I encourage anyone else to ask for). It was not something I expected, nor something I was asking God to give me.

When I got back to my mom's house, I talked privately with my wife about it and told her, "Karon, I think this was from God, but I may have just eaten too much pizza last night!" Months went by, and we were contacted by over twenty churches (I never solicited these contacts, nor did I ask anyone to help me make them; they just came from multiple directions and locations—to this day I have no idea how it all happened) to discuss me serving as senior pastor.

I would have conversations with their contact people, and Karon would say, "Rick, what about that vision?" My response was that if it were from God it would come to pass, and if it were my imagination then we didn't want it to happen.

Ultimately, some months later The Grace Place contacted us, and I responded to an invitation to serve as the pastor.

My wife and I have been at our current church for nearly three decades. During that time, many of the things I envisioned happening have happened, but I am confident that there is still more to come. I'm not sure how all of that is going to happen, nor when it will happen, but know God is going to bring it to pass.

With all the blessings, there have been many times that I have felt like Joseph must have felt when things were not going well for him. That vision of his family bowing down in front of him in fulfillment of that dream kept him optimistic and hopeful in the worst and the best of times.

The vision God gave me months prior to coming to serve at The Grace Place has kept me going when other people have thought I was not wise to take the stuff I did "on the chin" and keep on keeping on. By doing that, however, we have seen one rewarding result after another developing that God gave me a vision for nearly three decades ago.

Vision enables us to envision what God wants us to do so that nothing Satan throws at you will distract you from the great work God has for you to do!

Vision Killers

Many leaders struggle with finding a vision and how to go about putting it into place. Sometimes it is because they have allowed themselves to be controlled by what I call "vision killers"—obstacles they cannot seem to overcome, deep personal insecurities, being unable to step outside of their comfort zone, or being unable to be deeply committed to their ministry.

Tradition

I love traditions in my family. If you are like me, you probably find yourself saying things like, "Our family always does this at Christmastime!" "Every summer we go to the mountains/beach/shore!" "We always go to Grandmom's for Sunday brunch/tea/dinner." The list can just keep going on. Those traditions are wonderful to pass along to children and grandchildren for generations to come. They give continuity, security, and great memories. If you want to be a lionhearted leader and take your ministry to a place it has never been before though, traditions can kill fresh vision.

One of the most devastating barriers to true vision is the notion that God would never ask you do something different from what you have always done before. Good traditions can build a foundation upon which God can build for the future. God blesses those traditions, which build the church and His people because they serve His purposes. But God has no use for traditions that block progress.

Tradition is generally focused on the past, and vision is always a focus on the future. As a lionhearted leader, I know God wants to use the past to enhance our future. Early in my ministry journey my vision was trampled on by church old-timers who said, "We've never done it that way!" When I hear that these days, I am reminded of the adage that says: "The most basic definition of insanity is to keep doing the same thing over and over and expecting different results." A lionhearted leader will affirm the good that has occurred through the ways of the past but will be prepared to communicate how much better the future can be if we work together toward the common goal and vision!

Fear

Fear is a natural reaction when we face the challenge of doing something we have not done before. Lionhearted leaders will discover God is going to regularly challenge them to do something they have never done before.

The Bible tells the story of Joshua taking the reins of leadership when Moses dies. He knows God's calling to lead the Hebrews into the land of promise he had personally seen forty years earlier. He and Caleb were two of the twelve spies Moses had sent into the promised land to come back and tell them what they found. They gave a positive report and saw what other ten spies had seen as well. The ten negative spies said:

> But the men who had gone up with him said, "We can't attack those people; they are stronger than we are." And they spread among the Israelites a bad report about the land they had explored. They said, "The land we explored devours those living in it. All the people we saw there are of great size. We saw the Nephilim there

(the descendants of Anak come from the Nephilim). We seemed like grasshoppers in our own eyes, and we looked the same to them." (Numbers 13:31–33 NIV 2011)

In contrast Joshua and Caleb had a very different perspective on the challenges of possessing the land promised to them for the last four to five hundred years. This is their lionhearted reaction to the giants and walled cities:

They gave Moses this account: "We went into the land to which you sent us, and it does flow with milk and honey! Here is its fruit. But the people who live there are powerful, and the cities are fortified and very large. We even saw descendants of Anak there. The Amalekites live in the Negev; the Hittites, Jebusites and Amorites live in the hill country; and the Canaanites live near the sea and along the Jordan." Then Caleb silenced the people before Moses and said, "We should go up and take possession of the land, for we can certainly do it." (Numbers 13:27–30 NIV 2011)

Now, once again, after wandering in the wilderness for forty years, it is time for the Israelites to cross the flooded Jordan River and take possession of the land God had promised them for hundreds of years. Joshua is going to have put into practice what he said he believed forty years earlier. God comes to him and says:

After the death of Moses, the servant of the LORD, the LORD said to Joshua, son of Nun, Moses' aide: "Moses my servant is dead. Now then, you and all these people, get ready to cross the Jordan River into the land I am about to give to them—to the Israelites. I will give you every place where you set your foot, as I promised Moses. Your territory will extend from the desert to Lebanon, and from the great river, the Euphrates—all the Hittite country—to the Mediterranean Sea in the west. No one will be able to stand against you all the days of your life. As I was with Moses, so I will be with you; I will never leave you nor forsake you. Be strong and courageous, because you will lead these people to inherit the land, I swore to their ancestors to give them. "Be strong and very courageous. Be careful to obey all the law my servant Moses gave you; do not turn from it to the right or to the left, that you may be successful wherever you go. Keep this Book of the Law always on your lips; meditate on it day and night, so that you may be careful to do everything written in it. Then you will be prosperous and successful. Have I not commanded you? Be strong and courageous. Do not be afraid; do not be discouraged, for the LORD your God will be with you wherever you go." (Joshua 1:1–9 NIV 2011)

A lionhearted leader faces many different fears when God calls him to lead his people to places they have never been before. One of the fears I have dealt with is, *Can I convince people of the need, the opportunities, the future blessing to come if they decide to follow the vision?* Sometimes people who reject your vision will reject you at the same time. Every time you take on a new challenge, it will prod people out of their comfort zones. It always creates resistance, and sometimes that resistance causes them to reject the leader.

Another fear I always deal with is the fear of failure. Will we be able to recruit enough people to start this ministry? Can we raise the money to complete the project? How will people respond to the ministry or use the facility? How many unknown obstacles will we run into? Are we taking on more than we can afford? Those and a myriad of other questions will keep a lionhearted leader awake at night and dog their steps during the day.

Then we need to lean hard on God's promises just like Joshua did as he led the Hebrews into the Promised Land. God tells him multiple times: "Be strong and courageous, do not be afraid." I have made this statement over and over to our church: "when fear walks in the front door of your life, faith walks out the back door!" But when "faith walks in the front door of your life, fear walks out the back door!" Fear and faith cannot coexist at the same time in your life. The lionhearted leader will always be called by God to have the faith to believe God will do what has not ever been done before and take on challenges that other people declare to be impossible!

Many leaders are afraid they will lose control by expanding a ministry or developing an area of ministry where they need to recruit someone else to lead.

As C. Peter Wagner would say frequently about a church growing, the pastor must move from being a shepherd to becoming a rancher. It is easy to be afraid some of your people will develop loyalties to the leader of the ministry you are developing and diminish your influence in their lives. I believe that behind this fear for some is a narcissism that is characterized by selfishness, a sense of entitlement, and the need for admiration. Many leaders unfortunately possess this very destructive focus on their self-interest. I have discovered that I must always be ready to "give up to go up" with the development of the church. As I evaluate what I have given up to go up, the benefits have always exceeded the losses.

Complacency

Some of us do not want to be pushed out of our personal comfort zone, and we are okay with things the way they are. I call that complacency. Far too many pastors are content to preach a sermon or two a week, do an occasional funeral or wedding, draw their breath and a paycheck, and put the church on autopilot. I am not one of those kinds of guys. I have always felt like we are on a mission to take the good news of the gospel to anyone in our community who is far from God.

Many pastors are content with the status-quo and do not want to deal with the stress of stretching and growing if the church has enough money to pay their salary—enough people to have a little crowd to preach to, they see no reason to cause disruption and take the risk of developing anything.

Lionhearted leaders see people all around them who are in desperate need of a life-changing relationship with Jesus Christ. They will always be looking for and sensitized to the needs of people around them. They will then start thinking and praying about what God wants their church to do about reaching these people with the hope of the gospel.

Other pastors are complacent because they are lazy. They are not looking for anything that requires more work, energy, or time than they are already giving. I love pastors and do everything I can to encourage them in their ministry journey. In trying to coach them many times I have come to realize the real problem they have is a motivational one. You can help people who genuinely want to help themselves, but I don't know a cure for a lack of motivation.

I have always felt like the worst insult I could ever experience was to be called "lazy" by someone for whom I worked. When I was just a little boy, I remember my dad saying to me one day, "Rick, you are the hardest working little boy I have ever seen!" I have always enjoyed working and have been continuously employed since I was fourteen years old. I love to work and cannot imagine anything I would like less than to be retired. I have said many times that I want to work until the last day of my life.

There are also a lot of pastors who are complacent because they do not know where to start to bring about change. They do not read anything to challenge themselves to understand how to lead more effectively.

Many of them are afraid to interact with pastors who are doing things differently than they are. If you are not exposing yourself to people who are better than you are, whose experiences in ministry are different and larger than yours, you will keep doing the same thing over and over and getting the same results—and never figure out why. Read some good books, interact with other pastors, and you will discover as iron sharpens iron, these books and pastors will be used by God to stretch you mind, your faith, and your capabilities.

CHAPTER 10

Fighting Fatigue, Dreaming Big

Sometimes we experience fatigue because we are overworked and have not taken enough time to get adequate rest. Many times, when I feel I am losing my vision and focus it is because I have not taken enough time to refresh my body and my spirit.

For many years I would schedule breakfast and lunch meetings with people in the church, staff members, or other pastors nearly every day of the week. But it seemed I was always in a rush—like I was on a vicious treadmill that would not stop. About six months ago I realized the schedule was not only leaving me exhausted most of the time but was affecting my ability to see our next steps and move forward with the church. I now occasionally have a breakfast meeting, but never more than once a week, and it is generally with a pastor God is using to sharpen the edges of my life. It has had a lot of positive benefits in my life physically, emotionally, and spiritually and as a leader.

About fifteen years ago I had what I would call "a year of great distress!" We had a lot of personal family distraction with our two grown sons having issues in their lives beyond our control.

And to top it off, our church was in the middle of a major multimillion-dollar reconstruction, and I was trying to lead us through that project in the middle of an emotionally devastating time in my personal life.

Looking back on it, I realize we made some decisions with that project we would never have made if I had not been so emotionally drained by what we were dealing with in our personal life.

It is OK to push the pause button for a few months when you are exhausted by things over which you have no control. I must remind myself that Rome was not built in a day, and the kingdom of God is not either.

Short-Term Thinking

Short-term thinking will kill a vision every time. Many pastors are always looking for a "better" opportunity and only see where they are as a stepping stone to getting where they think they want to go.

The cure for short-term thinking is loyalty to your church and calling. Since coming to The Grace Place, I have never envisioned going anywhere else to serve as a pastor. I believe one of the reasons God has sustained my vision is because I love this church, our congregation, and our community, and would feel like I was abandoning them to go somewhere else.

We live in a time where commitment is a lost value. You see this lack in the casual attitude people have toward their marriages and jobs. I believe a loss of commitment is not only a problem with people in the church who are ready to exit if the church does not meet their expectations. It is also evident by the flippant attitudes toward the church many people have as well.

If you are going to have a sustained vision for your church, you must see it from the long haul, not for the short term. Vision for Joseph meant waiting over twenty years for his dream to become a reality. Joshua kept his vision alive for forty years wandering in the wilderness. Do not let the vision killers destroy your vision for the church you are leading.

A Better Future

Lionhearted leaders are not afraid to *dream some big dreams* and have the faith to believe God can help them to see those dreams come to fulfillment. That vision will cause a lionhearted leader to take "faith steps" into a future they have never experienced before. Those faith steps require a level of faith that believes God will enable them to do things other leaders say are impossible! There is nothing that has stretched and grown my faith like leading into territory I have never been in before.

When we were nearing the completion of our first major building project, I remember walking through the facility when it was about 90 percent complete, looking at the classrooms and the various parts of the building. We owed around half a million dollars on the facility, which at the time felt enormous!

I had this huge fear come over me that I know now came straight from Satan himself. The fear was, *You have led the church into this project, gotten them into debt, and now what if we can't fill up the facility?*

Many times since then, I have observed pastors who have led churches through building projects accumulate a lot of debt and then have this mysterious voice say, "God is calling me to go somewhere else." When I talk to them, I realize they were experiencing the same fear I felt. The difference is that a lionhearted leader believes if God has led them, then He will provide what is needed to experience the blessings and benefits of the vision He has given them.

The rest of the story is, we moved into that facility, and it has been used to the max now for over two-and-a-half decades.

Lionhearted leaders have a faith that is *not afraid to believe* God will do what needs to be done. Nothing starts happening until somebody starts dreaming. Every accomplishment starts off first as an idea in somebody's mind, a dream, a vision, or a goal. If you are not dreaming great dreams, envisioning new ministries, stretching your imagination as to what can be, then your goal will remain the status quo. Solomon says in Proverbs 29:18 (King James Version) *"Where there is no vision, the people perish."*

If your church does not have a vision, it will stay the same. I heard someone say: "If you aim at nothing, you are definitely going to hit it!" God has always led His people through the vision of the leader. That means your church's vision will never be greater than the vision of the pastor. If you are a pastor, it is imperative you have a God-given, God-directed vision for your church. I believe one of the primary tasks of ministry leadership is to establish a vision for your church. If you are not setting the vision, you are not the real leader of your church. A church will never outgrow its vision, and the vision of the church is never greater than the vision of the pastor.

The Benefits of a Clear Vision

Lionhearted leaders know *vision is a powerful tool* to grow people in their faith. One of the reasons God wants the leader to have clear vision is because it always challenges people's lives to be changed through faith in Christ.

A God-led, God-sized vision always will pull the church together and serve as a spiritual catalyst that moves the church forward collectively to accomplish something they have never experienced before. When a church buys into a vision, it brings unity, focus, direction, and enthusiasm and helps each person to know they are a part of something collectively that is greater than they will ever experience individually.

As we have led the church through each major project and the beginning of many different ministries, we have seen people grow in their faith to believe God for the impossible. In fact, we have challenged the church members to envision each of our major projects and see what happens in response to their vision. Some of our businesspeople will share with me how through those experiences they were able to envision greater opportunities to expand and grow their own businesses. Many of them have become successful because of the influence of the church and seeing how vision can impact their business lives.

Lionhearted leaders know *vision pulls people out of their lethargy.* There are always people in the church who seem complacent and nonmotivated. I have discovered when they see and buy into the church's vision, they just need someone else to see what they cannot and point them in the direction they need to go. Frequently the uninspired will start serving with enthusiasm all because the vision ignited something in them that pulls them out of their lethargy and noninvolvement.

Lionhearted leaders know *vision will inspire people to give generously.* When a God-led, God-inspired vision captures peoples' hearts, and they understand the benefits, they are moved to give toward a better future that will be the product of the vision!

I believe that most people want to be a part of something bigger than they are and reach people in our communities they have not yet reached. A vision enables them to see how that can come to pass, and it will inspire them to sacrificial generosity.

Lionhearted leaders focus their leadership energy on accomplishing the vision or the goal. President John Kennedy inspired a nation to believe we could put a man on the moon by the end of the 1960s. That vision focused the energy of NASA to work tirelessly to accomplish that goal in 1969 when we landed the first man on the moon. His vision focused the energy of an entire government agency to accomplish what seemed impossible at the time!

A church without a focused vision can be like a person chasing rabbits. You are running in multiple directions, making quick changes, and coming up empty-handed. You expend a great deal of energy with little results.

A great vision clarifies the direction, focuses on the target, and looks for specific results. When it is communicated well, everyone knows the goal.

Lionhearted leaders know vision is *key to developing momentum.* Progress requires intentionality toward the envisioned outcome. Vision is always required to move even a small group of people forward. In fact, I think vision is required no matter the size of the group.

Vision Cannot Be Delegated

I can always compensate for my weaknesses—can always hire people to do things or delegate to volunteers the things that I cannot do. If I am not good at counseling, I can find people who are good at counseling. If I am not good at administration and details, I can find people to handle administration and details.

But there is one thing I cannot delegate. *I cannot ask other people to believe God for me.* I must set the pace in terms of vision, dreams, and faith. You cannot delegate faith in God. The Bible tells us in Proverbs 11:27 (NLT): "Be wise, my child, and make my heart glad. Then I will be able to answer my critics."

Lionhearted leaders are not afraid to dream great dreams for God.

One nice thing about dreams is you can think through them, pray through them, and it does not cost you anything at all. The Bible says, "God is able to do far more than we would ever dare to ask or even dream of —infinitely beyond our highest prayers, desires, thoughts, or hopes" (Ephesians 3:20 TLB). God says (paraphrased), "Think up the biggest thing you think I can do in your life, in your ministry, in your church—and I can top that. I can beat it."

A lionhearted leader will ask this question: "What would I attempt for God if I knew I couldn't fail?" Every time I ask myself that question it expands my horizons, unleashes my dreams, and expands my vision. It starts with a dream.

Three Key Questions

So many people have no idea how to even start finding a vision for their ministry. I have discovered there are three key questions I need to ask myself if I am going to find the vision God wants me to have for my church or organization.

First, ask God to show you the answer to the question "What?" When I start there, I discover after praying and meditating for a while, He shows me what He's going to do.

The big mistake we make once we have a sense of what God wants to do is trying to accomplish it on our own. Inevitably we fall flat on our faces and come crawling back to God saying, "Oh, God. I'm so sorry. What did I do? Did I miss the vision? You told me what you were going to do, and I went out and tried to accomplish it and fell flat on my face. Did I miss something?" And God will say to you, "No, you didn't. You just didn't wait for part two."

When God shows you what He wants you to do, you have wait to find the answer to the second question: "How do you want me to do it?" I have discovered when God shows you how, it always seems to be the opposite way from that which you thought.

When God led Joshua and the Hebrews to defeat the city of Jericho, God's "how" seemed to be absurd. When he called Gideon to defeat the great armies, God's "how" just did not make sense. All through the Bible, God's "how" has flown in the face of conventional wisdom and practices.

God's vision always involves timing, and that leads us to the third question: "When?" The Bible tells us there is a right time for everything under the sun.

The longer that I'm alive and the longer I walk with the Lord and the longer I'm in ministry, the more I'm convinced that God's timing is perfect. He is never a minute early, and he is never a minute late; he is always right on time.

These are the three parts to getting God's vision: what, how, and when. And you must wait for all three parts for God to work in your life.

Key Takeaway

Some of us need to stop praying for God to bless what we are doing and focus on doing the things that He is blessing.

Always ask God, "What do you want me to do? How do you want me to do it? And when do you want me to do it?" Just tell God you want to focus on what He is doing and blessing!

Lionhearted leaders know God will always use the person who has a dream. Pray God will give you a great vision and a great dream and then strengthen you to fulfill it.

CHAPTER 11

Lionhearted Goals

God-given goals will stretch your faith. Therefore, lionhearted pastors always seeks God-given goals for their ministry. The true church will claim territory for God that breaks Satan's strongholds in people's lives. Every ministry God is using today in our church started off as a dream, a vision, and then ultimately a goal.

If you do not have goals for your church, your default goal is to remain the same. The lionhearted pastor understands the church's goals will never be larger than his vision. You cannot delegate your vision, your faith, and your courage to someone else.

The lionhearted pastor will dream bold and audacious dreams and then believe God will do even greater things. Apostle Paul says in Ephesians 3:20 (LB), "God is able to do far more than we would ever dare to ask or even dream of; infinitely beyond our highest prayers, desires, thoughts, or hopes." Basically, God says, "Think up the biggest thing you think I can do in your life, in your ministry, in your church, and I can top that." Do not limit God by small and ineffective visions and dreams.

The Benefits of Goals

Goals are a road map toward a better future. God-given goals dramatically increase the chances of the church arriving at the right destination. Everybody ends up somewhere in life, but only a few people get there on purpose. Those are the ones with the right goals. Having clear goals, along with the courage to follow through, dramatically increases your chances of coming to the end of your life, looking back with deep satisfaction, and saying "I did it! I succeeded! I finished well! My life mattered!"

Without clear goals, odds are you will come to the end of your life and wonder what you could have and should have done. You may wonder if your life really mattered at all.

Goals Make the Mundane Matter

Goals give significance to otherwise meaningless details of our ministries. The details, chores, and routines of life then become a worthwhile means to a planned-for end. Much of what we do doesn't appear to matter when evaluated apart from some larger context or purpose. Take the minutia of this very day, drop it into the cauldron of God-ordained goals, stir it around, and suddenly there is purpose, meaning, adrenaline!

It is like the difference between filling bags with dirt and building a dike to save a town. There is nothing glamorous or fulfilling about filling bags with dirt. But saving a town is another thing altogether. Building a dike gives meaning to the chore of filling bags with dirt. And so it is with vision.

Focused Goals Motivate People

When men or women lack motivation, it is because they have little goals or no goals at all. They may have ideas, and they may have dreams, but ideas and dreams are not goals.

Having goals is a big part of why you complete college or graduate school. A lack of goals is the reason many never finish. Think of all the seemingly wasted hours of study and class time. You may think what you are memorizing for tests is a waste of time and effort, but you do it anyway. Why? Because of what could be. A degree. And beyond a degree, a career. For four (or in my case, five and a half) years, you endure science labs, European history, research papers, and lectures. You hang in there through it all, motivated by the thought of graduation and the rewards it will bring. That is the power of setting and achieving goals.

Goals Generate Passion

There is no such thing as an emotionless goal. Think about your daydreams. The thing that makes daydreaming so enjoyable is the emotion that piggybacks on the images of your mind.

When we allow our thoughts to wander outside the walls of reality, our feelings are quick to follow. A clean, focused goal allows us to experience ahead of time the emotions of hope and happiness associated with our anticipated future. These emotions serve to reinforce our commitment and provide a sneak preview of what's to come. The feelings reserved for tomorrow are brought into our present reality.

Goals Simplify Decision-Making

Anything that moves us toward the realization of our goals gets a green light. Everything else is approached with caution.

I am always amazed at how difficult it is for churches to make decisions. When you analyze the reasons for a church's indecision, it is generally because it has never taken the time to figure out where it is going and what it wants to accomplish.

When we set our goals, we know what we are planning to do for a year to three years ahead, and we generally have no problem in making decisions.

Goals Help Prioritize Your Values

Clear goals have the power to bring what's most important into focus. Clear goals make it easy to weed out those things that stand in the way of achieving what matters most. Goals help us to keep our focus on the main thing and not a million different things that don't make a difference.

There are always people hanging around the fringes of the church who have strange ideas about what the church "should" be doing.

When you know what your goals are, you can respond like this: "That is a good idea, but it doesn't fit into the goals we believe God wants us to focus on developing." It doesn't always make them happy, but it is a great tool to communicate your values to people who have questionable agendas.

Goals Empower You to Move Purposefully in a Predetermined Direction

Once you have clarified your goals, many decisions are already made. Without clearly defined goals, good things will hinder you from achieving the best things. My observation is that people without clear goals are easily distracted. They tend to drift from one activity, pleasure, or relationship to another.

Without clearly defined goals, there is no relational, financial, or moral compass. Consequently, we often make foolish decisions that rob us of our dreams.

Goals Enable You to Fulfill God's Purpose for the Church

Goals give you a reason to get up in the morning. If you don't show up, something important won't be accomplished. Suddenly, you matter a lot! Without you, what could be or should be will not be. God-inspired goals help us see we are an important link between current reality and the future.

Purpose carries with it the momentum to move you through barriers that would otherwise slow you down and trip you up.

Goals Challenge You to Take on Bold Initiatives

Goals will challenge those we lead to a new level of achievement. God-inspired goals force you to do things you have never done before and to take on projects you would have delayed.

Goals Provide You with Long-Range Focus

Goals linked with strategic planning require looking ahead one year or three years or longer. They keep you from being constantly distracted by the pressures of the immediate. I know many pastors who are busy but who never accomplish their goals or anything of significance for that matter.

Goals Transform the Future

Helen Keller was asked, "What would be worse than being born blind?" She replied, "To have sight without vision." Because of God-inspired goals, there is a very clear connection between where The Grace Place is today and where the church was when we came in 1993. Because of God-given goals, we have developed life-changing ministries, reached people far from God, baptized many believers, and built over $10 million worth of buildings.

I have always looked at ministry as an opportunity to reach out to people and connect with them where they are. By developing ministries to which people respond, we can bring them into the family of God. As a result, we always keep our eyes open for needs, opportunities, and challenges in our community and around the world.

We have been involved in our community with outreach through ministries such as Celebrate Recovery, Divorce Care, Grief Share, and then basics of having a food pantry available to those in need. The church has also sponsored me to go to Bolivia, South America, and Spain to teach leadership principles to church and business leaders. This has been very fulfilling but also taxing because they were three-year commitments. We have gone to other third world countries and shared the gospel and leadership principles there as well.

Important Facts about Goals

Goals Must Be Specific

Goals must be written out, or they are simply just ideas. Get it down in black and white on paper or use a computer. However you write it down, make sure it is printed and states what you are planning to accomplish. Having it written out is a consistent reminder of what should be focused on next.

A generalized plan may be easy to formulate, but objectives are easier to define when the goal is specific. A good goal is not saying, "We want our church to grow," but instead "We want the church to grow by a hundred people in the next twelve months."

Goals Must Be Realistic

In setting realistic goals, take time to identify possible and probable challenges. Think of potential obstacles so you can develop ways to overcome them. Imagine a "worst case scenario" and how you would respond. With planning and forethought, you can avoid many obstacles that would normally take up your time.

It may be exhilarating at first when you set lofty goals, but you need to remember that a goal that is impossible to reach is demoralizing. Setting realistic goals does not mean you should not stretch your imagination, resources, and previous experiences. The challenge for most of us is to find the balance between realistic and unrealistic goals. Many times, we are either setting the bar so high no one believes we can jump over it or setting the goal so low it does not stretch us or challenge us.

Goals Must Be Measurable

A measurable goal is important because it allows you to evaluate how well we are doing and is essential for you to see how you are progressing.

Measurable means knowing where you currently are and then determining what you want the increase to be. If you want to increase small group participation, then identify how many groups you have, what kind of new groups you need to start, and the number of additional people you want to see participating in those groups.

Goals Must Connect at the Heart Level

To inspire and motivate, we must have a clear understanding of the vision. It is not enough to understand it; we must connect emotionally with the vision. Once you own the vision, it is easier to inspire others to buy into the goals you have established.

When our goals connect on the heart level, the benefits of accomplishing them must be worth the effort and energy. Strategic goals will always push us out of our comfort zones, force us to do things we haven't done before, and make us work harder than ever. The desired outcomes must be seen as worth the energy and effort they require the team to make.

Goals Must Have Supporting Strategies

Without predetermined strategies to accomplish it, a goal is just a lofty idea. That is why I always refer to our goal-setting time as "Goals and

Strategies" meetings. In our strategic planning sessions, we generally only have three or four goals but will have dozens of strategies focused on how we can accomplish each goal. Many times, those strategies involve everything from advertising to building a building. In fact, we have never made a building project a goal. The buildings have always been a strategy to accomplish a larger goal.

One of the churches I pastored prior to coming to The Grace Place made constructing a new building their primary goal. The pastor who led them through the construction project resigned within a year of completion. I believe it was primarily because finishing the building made him believe he'd accomplished what he came here to do.

The church floundered because it had not developed a ministry objective to fill the building up when it was completed. I learned from that ministry experience to never let facilities be the goal, just a strategy to accomplish a ministry objective. So, all three of our major facilities (totaling more than 55,000 square feet) we have built over three decades of ministry at The Grace Place were not "goals." They have all been a part of a strategy to facilitate developing ministries to reach people where they are.

All Goals and Strategies Must Be Clearly Communicated

Communication is sharing a vision of the objective that is to be accomplished. Clarification is showing the steps that need to be followed. This does not mean specifically telling someone what to do.

The best plan is useless unless the leader can communicate it in a way that challenges people's imagination and helps them see what looks impossible as being possible. Our best buy-in to the church's vision has occurred when I have been able to clearly articulate what we are doing, why we are doing it, and what we anticipate accomplishing by working together to bring this vision into a future reality.

Nehemiah was successful in rebuilding the walls of Jerusalem because he knew what he wanted to do, when he wanted to do it, and had the courage to keep on keeping on no matter what obstacles he encountered. His passion for the project motivated those he pulled together to do what seemed to be a nearly impossible job in a very short period.

Let the Size of Your God Determine the Size of Your Goals

- **Christian goal setting is based on the promises of God.**

Find a promise you can claim from God's word. Do not worry about the "how." Do not worry about current problems. Just believe God will do what he says He will do. If God said He will do it, then it is something you can claim in faith believing He will come through. In both the Old and New Testament, those God used most effectively are those who had a vision from God and the faith to believe He would do what He said He would do. Whether it was Moses leading the Hebrews toward the Promised Land, Joshua conquering the Promised Land, or Paul's Macedonian Vision, when they had a vision from God, they also had the audacity to believe He would do what He said He would do.

- **Christian goal setting is focused on the power of God.**

Here is the difference between Christian and non-Christian goal setting. The Christian doesn't just look at his or her own resources and talent and say, "What can I accomplish?" There are over seven thousand promises in the Bible. The real issue is not "Who do I think I am? It is who do I think God is?"

A lionhearted pastor knows you have never really trusted God until you've attempted something that can't be done in your own strength and resources.

We have a motto at The Grace Place that states this attitude clearly: "Only God!" Every day, I hear people in our church use that expression in conversations to describe something amazing God has done. I see it in their social media posts, text messages, and emails. The lionhearted leader recognizes "Only God" can do the things everyone else says are impossible. We adopted that motto because I want people to expect God to come through and do the supernatural. That creates a "can do" kind of attitude, and it keeps the naysayers in the minority.

- **Pray for God's blessing on your goals.**

Jesus tells us: "Therefore I tell you, whatever you ask in prayer, believe that you have received it, and it will be yours" (Mark 11:24 ESV).

And David tells us, "Delight yourself in the Lord and He'll give you the desires of your heart" (Psalm 37:4 ESV) and "No good thing will He withhold from them who walk uprightly" (Psalm 84:11 ESV).

We are repeatedly told in scripture to pray not just for our needs but also for our desires. We are told to pray for these things because prayer purifies our desires. It distinguishes between a whim or wish and a deep desire. Many times, God seems to delay the answer to our prayer because he wants to test the depth of our desires. Are we serious? Praying about our goals and plans is a declaration of dependence on God!

- **Evaluate the benefits versus the cost.**

There are always problems and obstacles to overcome to reach your goals. You will go through tough times.

My experiences tell me that if you don't know why you want what you want, if you don't foresee a payoff or reward, if you don't know what the benefits are going to be, you're going to give up when things get tough.

Anything great ever accomplished has always required sacrifices of time, energy, money, effort, and reputation. There's always a payment. Many people today want to reach their goal only if it's convenient. "I've always wanted to be a writer … be a singer … start this hobby … I'm going to do it in my spare time. One of these days I'm going to get around to it."

- **Develop a strategic plan.**

Reaching your goals requires taking proactive steps toward those goals. A strategic plan is simply a predetermined course of action. You plan out a course of action, and you write down your specific steps to implement it. Then you set a deadline, and you schedule it.

- **Put together an action and planning calendar.**

The action and planning calendar identifies when a project is to be completed and determines when the assigned person or persons need to start working on the project to complete it in time. If the goal is to be implemented in July, then the action part of it must start months before the implementation date. If you do not have the start date on the calendar, the date to begin the ministry will come and go and never get off the ground.

The action and planning calendar requires a mental walk-through. You must mentally walk through the entire goal or event you are planning and note anything you might have forgotten. For us that means I must sit down with my assistant and work through what we have overlooked in the strategic planning event. Many times, implementing a goal requires recruiting the right people, buying the right equipment, selecting the right materials, or working with a designer to put together the plans. Other times, it requires a fund-raising strategy or campaign to fund the project.

The action and planning calendar is taking "the next steps" to determine the immediate action you must take to accomplish your goal. Some of the best goals and strategies we have ever developed did not get implemented because we waited too long to start taking the next steps needed to see them come together.

The action and planning calendar is one of the most important results of any strategic planning meeting.

- **Adjust for unanticipated opportunities and obstacles.**

A river constantly changes course and is never the same as it was before, and ministries are the same. Regardless of how conscientiously plans are made, there is a constant need for monitoring and correction if the destination is to be reached. I say always have a plan but have the understanding that when you stop adjusting and making changes, your course will be altered, and you will get off track.

- **Develop a system to "keep score" of the results.**

"Keeping score" is the only way to know if you're winning or losing. Use anything from a legal pad to a computer database program to write down where you are in the process of achieving your goals. If you're making a change, you ought to do it based on current information. Remember:

Goals are a must for any lionhearted leader.
Goals must be God-centered.
Goals must be measured in time.
Goals must have flexibility built in.
Goals must give room for specific strategies.

CHAPTER 12

Lionhearted Planning

One of the great visionary leaders in the Old Testament was King Solomon. Solomon did not ask for great riches or fame for himself, but rather he asked for wisdom so he could lead God's people. Solomon demonstrates a key aspect of leadership—knowing where you want to go before asking others to follow you. In 2 Chronicles 1:10 (NIV) he prays: "Give me wisdom and knowledge, that I may lead this people, for who is able to govern this great people of yours?"

Once your personal and organizational mission is defined, the methods become easier to clarify as well. Solomon knew the key to great planning is focus. All great human endeavors have always included a God factor and a leadership factor. God has given us lionhearted leaders a mission that requires vision and planning on our part.

Strategic planning is the road you follow to make dreams become a reality. It is the process where ideas and convictions take on substance.

God gives us the best example of planning. "Have you not heard? Long ago I did it, from ancient times I planned it. Now I have brought it to pass" (Isaiah 27:26 NIV). You cannot look at creation without realizing our God is a "planner." He planned this world and all of creation to function with balance and beauty. When sin entered the world, God had a plan from the "foundations of the earth" to send Jesus as the Redeemer of a lost creation.

God had done some long-range planning before He gave Moses the detailed instructions (plans) for building the tabernacle. When it was completed, it was perfect. It never needed to be altered or increased in size.

Nehemiah's Model for Strategic Planning

Nehemiah and the rebuilding of the wall around Jerusalem are patterns for planning. Nehemiah had a vision of seeing the walls of Jerusalem rebuilt. He put together plans for its construction. Because of his planning, he was able to rebuild the walls in just fifty-two days. Some key ingredients in Nehemiah's plan and his approach to planning clarify God's process in effective planning:

Identify the problem.

Nehemiah saw the problem. "They said to me, 'Those who survived the exile and are back in the province are in great trouble and disgrace. The wall of Jerusalem is broken down, and its gates have been burned with fire'" (Nehemiah 1:3 NIV).

Nehemiah could have dismissed this report. He could have said, "Too bad, what a tragic ending for the once glorious city of David." He could have said, "I am cupbearer in Persia now, and my career and destiny is there." Nehemiah was the kind of Jew who said, in Psalm 137:5–6 (ESV): "If I forget you O Jerusalem let my right hand forget her cunning. Let my tongue cleave to the roof of my mouth, if I remember not you above my chief joy."

Seek God's direction before planning.

Nehemiah sought God's direction before he started planning. "When I heard these things, I sat down and wept. For some days I mourned and fasted and prayed before the God of heaven" (Nehemiah 1:4 NIV). Nehemiah was touched in his heart. It is obvious that, had Nehemiah's heart not melted or been moved, he never would have had the courage to work as he did to rebuild the walls. "For some days I … fasted and prayed before the God of heaven."

Nehemiah teaches us we will never be successful in working for God until we are quiet before Him. It is in the quietness of solitude that God speaks. Over the past couple of decades, God has shown me in a variety of ways that if I am ever going to do anything to make an eternal difference, it must start with prayer and fasting. That is why from time to time after seeing the problem, I will go on a personal spiritual retreat. When I do, I spend the entire day fasting and praying for God's specific leadership and His plan to emerge. I have no interest in just putting a plan together. It must be His plan!

Evaluate the options.

Nehemiah surveyed the situation and spent time evaluating the options before he took any action toward rebuilding. After arriving in Jerusalem and resting for three days, he goes out by night to survey the damage. He does not tell anyone why he has come or what his plans are until after he knows what he wants to do.

> I set out during the night with a few men … By night I
> went out through the Valley Gate toward the Jackal Well
> and the Dung Gate, examining the walls of Jerusalem,

which had been broken down, and its gates, which had been destroyed by fire. Then I moved on toward the Fountain Gate and the King's Pool, but there was not enough room for my mount to get through; so I went up the valley by night, examining the wall. Finally, I turned back and reentered through the Valley Gate. (Nehemiah 2:12–15 NIV)

"Surveying" for us means conducting demographic studies and congregational interviews, evaluating special needs in our community, identifying unique opportunities, etc.

Gain support.

Nehemiah was able to motivate others to support the plan.

> Then I said to them, "You see the trouble we are in: Jerusalem lies in ruins, and its gates have been burned with fire. Come, let us rebuild the wall of Jerusalem, and we will no longer be in disgrace." I also told them about the gracious hand of my God on me and what the king had said to me. They replied, "Let us start rebuilding." So, they began this good work. (Nehemiah 2:17–18)

After being quiet before God, receiving his instructions and analyzing the need, he appears before the city council. After presenting the need and his plan to meet it, they in essence said, "Let's get on with the program."

Implement the plan.

Nehemiah formulated a plan and set about to implement it. After seeing the need (the walls were in ruins), seeking God's direction, and surveying the situation, Nehemiah put together a plan of action that enabled him to rebuild the walls in just fifty-two days.

> I had not told anyone what my God had put in my heart to do for Jerusalem ... the officials did not know where I had gone or what I was doing, because as yet I had said nothing to the Jews or the priests or nobles or officials or any others who would be doing the work. (Nehemiah 2:12, 16 NIV)

Preparation for the Strategic Planning Event

- ### Evaluate your current circumstances.

The first question you need to ask is, "Where are we right now?" If I were to call you from my cell phone and say, "I want to come over to your house," the first thing you'd say is "Where are you right now?" Once you know where I am, then you can give me directions on how to get where I want to be and roughly when I would get there. I believe one of the hardest things for churches and pastors to do is honestly look at where they are and acknowledge things must change for the church to move forward. Many of us are so insecure we believe the evaluation of the present will cause us to lose credibility. Your people already know things are not going well whether you want to admit it or not.

Take the time to write down a list of the positive and the negative things going on in your church right now. Evaluate the effectiveness of current ministries and what needs to change. Look at your facilities and ask yourself: "Are we ready for company?" It takes maturity to be able to identify where you are right now, and it is essential if you are going to know what to include in your strategic plan.

The second question to ask is: "What do we need to change?" No matter how large a church is, there are always areas of ministry that need to change for it to grow. No church or ministry is perfect. There is always something that needs to be tweaked, adjusted, or overhauled. Some of us have "pet" ministries, things we started years ago, and we are afraid we will have to admit failure of some sort if we touch or change it.

The moment you stop setting goals and reaching for them, you're dying. Whether you've got a day, a year, or fifty years left, you ought to have a goal for tomorrow, next week, and next year. We either advance or decline. We choose life or death for our church by our willingness to change and grow.

- **Evaluate where your ministry currently is from as many angles as possible.**

A plan based on an unrealistic view of the present will lead to disaster. One way to verify that we are seeing the situation clearly is to look at it from different angles. God gave us two eyes for a reason. Two eyes give depth—each eye sees the picture from a different angle. A lionhearted pastor gains a clear idea of the present situation by looking at it from as many angles as possible.

- **Evaluate how people who are a part of your ministry see the ministry.**

As the leader make sure you regularly meet with people informally, perhaps over coffee, lunch, or dinner. Some churches use purchased evaluation tools to solicit information from their members. Most of the these "tools," however, cause more problems by far than they ever solve.

At one point I brought in a high-priced consultant. This guy created more problems than you can imagine and did more to damage the church than heal it. Most consultants come with "questionnaires" they use with every church, never taking the time to figure out the DNA of each church. I have never seen a consultant do much to move a church in the right direction. Consultants generally do not have a clear understanding of the church (even though they act like they do), and they do not attempt to understand the dynamics of your community. From my personal experience and those of a lot of pastors I network with, the outcomes are consistently negative.

Remember, God has called you to the ministry you serve today because he wants you to take time and expend the effort to understand your people and your community.

- **Evaluate how people in your community see your ministry.**

Keep your ears and eyes open when you are out and about in the community. Get to know guests and recent attendees. They can give you insights into what people in the community are saying about your church.

Not long ago I had a conversation with a recent attendee at one of our New Members dinners. He told me about a conversation he had with a lady friend over lunch. When she asked him where he was going to church, she said, "Oh yes, that is the homeless peoples' church." I have no idea where that came from. We make no respective of people who attend our church. We believe and attempt to function like everyone is created in God's image, so we are going to do our best to treat the wealthy, the educated, and the homeless the same.

•   **Evaluate what your statistics say is going on in your ministry.**

Make sure you know what attendance and giving patterns are saying about the overall direction of your ministry. Solomon says: "Know well the condition of your flock and pay attention to your herds." (Proverbs 27:23 ESV)

I attended one of Pastor Rick Warren's Purpose Driven Pastor's Conferences when his church, Saddleback, was celebrating their thirty-fifth anniversary. Because they have kept such good records, he was able to share exactly how many people were baptized, went on mission trips, and have been on ministry teams they have sent to all 198 nations in the world. It is no wonder Saddleback has been so powerfully used by God to advance the kingdom. I left that conference saying, "we have to do a better job of keeping track of vital statistics."

•   **Establish the right objectives.**

It is important to start by clearly defining your purposes. If you have not established your purposes for the church, then you have no clear idea where you are going. Rick Warren has done an excellent job with Saddleback Church, and I believe one of the keys to the church's effectiveness is because early on he established the five purposes they have as a church. He continually focuses on those purposes to ensure everyone attending the church knows why they exist.

Clearly defining your purposes helps determine what you want and don't want. You will never reach a vague goal. Vague goals do not attract; they do not draw. For example, you might say, "One of my goals is to travel." I ask where. You might say, "I want to increase my income." I ask, how much? You might say, "I want to start a new career." I ask, "what kind?" You might say, "I want to read the Bible." I say "when?" You might say, "I want to witness." I ask, "to whom?" You might say, "I want to lose weight." I ask, "how much?"

If you wait to solve all the problems in your life before you make the decision, you'll never decide.

- **Schedule a time to plan.**

A frequent mistake churches make is the failure to follow this step. A certain amount of time and energy must be allotted in the weekly agenda for the planning process. Everyone agrees strategic planning is important, but we often feel we're wasting time when we take long hours to do it. When very little planning happens, it takes more time for execution due to changes and unexpected events. When a good deal of time is spent planning, we will save time on the overall task.

- **Identify the overall objectives of your strategic plan.**

Make sure to develop a strategic plan that enables the church to *function with purpose and in harmony within the biblical model.* It is foundational for the leader to know the biblical model the first generation was focused on. That means knowing the answers to the questions:

What outreach ministries did that church have?
What discipleship ministries did that church have?
What activities did that church engage in?

Identify ministries God can use to reach people who are far from God in your community. You must be engaged in your community to be able to identify those needed ministries. Make it a practice to not duplicate a ministry another church is already doing.

God has blessed our church with a wonderful Celebrate Recovery program, and many thousands of people have been impacted by this ministry. As a result, over a half a dozen churches have started their own Celebrate Recovery ministries. Every time we hear about another church starting a Celebrate Recovery program I always say, "imitation is the sincerest form of flattery." Still, it does not change the reality that slicing the pie into smaller pieces does not make the pie larger. We do our best not to let that happen in our strategic planning. If we really want to see the kingdom of God advance, then we must be careful about not letting imitation happen in our ministries.

- **Include the staff in developing the strategic so they will have a sense of ownership.**

If the leader develops the plan on his own, then there is very little "buy-in," and no one feels ownership of the plan. When you develop the plan like I am describing, the chances are dramatically increased there will be much wider support for the plan.

The Strategic Planning Event

- **Key elements in a planning retreat/session:**

Hold a strategic planning meeting at a place other than on the church property to keep focused on developing the plan. If you attempt to meet at your church facilities, staff members might go to their offices, get distracted, and lose their focus on the plan.

I ask everyone to turn off their phones and wait for our breaks to turn them back on to get their messages. If someone's phone rings in the middle of the meeting, everyone is looking to see if the call is for them. Then, the person receiving the call walks out of the room, and everyone is wondering what it's about.

Satan knows a good strategic plan will invade his territory, and he will do everything he can to cause the group to lose focus.

- **Key people to include in the planning retreat/session:**

We include our elders (board members if you don't have elders) and their spouses, as well as all staff members. Each year, we also invite several key and highly committed ministry volunteers. We have discovered the importance of inviting special guests in their twenties or thirties or any other age group that may be underrepresented.

- **Necessary resources:**

  - Large post-it note sheets and an easel
  - Different colored markers
  - Projector or flat-screen TV
  - Computer
  - Refreshments
  - Arrangements for meals to be prepared and served

We always have someone inputting the ideas and ultimately the plan into a computer, so we don't lose any of the data. That info can be seen on the large flatscreen. To make it possible for the group in the room to keep their focus, the large "post-it" sheets are very helpful. When we fill up a sheet with dreams, goals, and strategies, they are stuck to the walls. After we are done the "dreaming" part, those sheets are there for everyone to see, and if a dream fits into the plan as a strategy, the whole group can envision it and interact on it.

We use different colored markers for the dreams, goals, and strategies. Those help the group to not get confused by what is on the large "post-it" sheets.

We take a twenty-minute morning and afternoon break. The refreshments are a help in keeping everyone's energy up and their focus on putting together the plan. Sometimes we have a lunch catered to us, or I take the group out to a nice restaurant.

- **The strategic planning meeting:**

Worship. It is especially important for the participants to keep a clear God focus in the whole planning process. If God's power and abilities to do the impossible are not kept in clear focus, then the group starts thinking and planning in extremely limited ways. Great plans are focused on what God can do—not what we can do.

Caring and sharing. Everyone comes to these meetings carrying burdens with them. It may be heartbreak over a child who is on a self-destructive path, a health need or concern, or a debilitating financial problem. If I am aware of the problem, and it is not confidential, I will ask them to share it with the group. We then open it up for anyone to share a special need in their lives. If you can get the distractions out of the way for the day, everyone is able to better engage with the group when they know they have support from those participating.

Vision Challenge. It is important to hear what God says about what He can do if we trust Him to do things everyone else says is impossible. Those vision challenges are frequently used by God to shift the focus toward Him and what He has done for those who come to Him with the challenges and needs they have.

Positive Highlights. It is important to identify the ministries where a lot of positive development is taking place. Highlight the wonderful things going on in those areas of ministry. Frequently, I will remind the group what we envisioned for a particular ministry five years ago and then we look at what God is doing through that ministry. It helps the group focus on identifying another area of need and developing a ministry to respond to that need.

Positive Statistics. If your organization grew by 20 percent last year, focus on the growth and then ask the group to help you analyze why that has happened. It will then inspire the group to think of other ways to accelerate further growth.

Dreaming. We lay ground rules as we start to dream:

1. There are no impossible dreams.
2. There is no making fun of any dream.
3. There are no discouraging statements made, eyes rolled, sighs, etc.
4. There is no defensiveness if we do not utilize a dream for the strategic plan.

Without those ground rules, people will be afraid to share a dream because they don't want it devalued.

Ask the group, "If we had no financial limitations, no staffing limitations, and no facility limitations, what kind of church would you dream we would look like? What kinds of ministries, facilities, growth, and outcomes would you dream of us having?"

Write down all the dreams on the post-it sheets in no order. List them just as they are expressed. Once a sheet is filled, then stick it on the wall and enter the information in the computer.

- **Developing goals and strategies**

Once the dreaming is exhausted, then take time to look over all the sheets on the walls and ask this question: "Which of these dreams do you think should move from a dream to a ministry strategy?" Then put a check mark by those the team thinks would work.

Once the dreams are checked, then start looking at several different goal areas that would support those dreams. Start working through each of those areas (again writing them on the post-it sheets) and putting them on the walls with each of the potential goal areas being put together. Open it up for additional input the entire time, always emphasizing that there are no bad ideas.

Once the strategies for the potential goal areas are identified and the strategies are defined, then prioritize the goals and strategies by numbering them. Go through the strategies and identify the best implementation dates for the strategies if the goal is to be achieved.

Within two weeks of the planning session, the pastor and staff need to work through refining the strategies, tweaking the development dates, and putting the action and planning calendar together.

When Walt Disney was building Disneyland, he went against the advice of advisers and architects, and first built the now famous gigantic castle in the middle of the park before building any infrastructure. Why? So, workers and employees would have a vision of what the finished Disneyland would look like.

CHAPTER 13

The Courage of a Lionhearted Leader

Your enemy shakes hands and greets you like an old friend, all the while conniving against you. When he speaks warmly to you, don't believe him for a minute; he's just waiting for the chance to rip you off. No matter how cunningly he conceals his malice, eventually his evil will be exposed in public. (Proverbs 26:24–26 MSG)

Ministry Storms:

Lionhearted pastors/leaders are going to deal with a variety of "ministry storms." They can range from terrifying (like a Category Five hurricane) to a frustrating inconvenience (like a rainy and dreary day). It is helpful to be emotionally prepared to deal with the inevitable ministry storms all of us deal with from time to time.

As much as we would prefer our ministry experience to be filled with days of sunshine and gentle breezes, it is just not the reality when you are in church ministry for decades. It is inevitable a lionhearted pastor will have to deal with some exceedingly difficult and dark storms.

1. Ministry is not for the faint-hearted.

Ministries' Dreary and Rainy Days

When we were serving the church in Findlay, Ohio, there were times in the winter months when there would be days of drizzling rain and dreary conditions. I called those the "drizzly and dreary days of winter." It didn't rain hard, the wind did not blow furiously, but after three or four days of it, your spirit started reflecting the dark and drizzly conditions outside. I would call those the "discouraging times in ministry."

One of Satan's most effective tools for shortening a pastor's ministry is discouragement. I have had hundreds of pastors talk to me about their churches, and many of them have said virtually the same thing: "Rick, I am so discouraged I do not think I can continue to move forward." Those are the times when a lionhearted pastor will grab himself by his own collar and say to himself, "I am not going to allow discouragement destroy what God has planned for me."

Discouragement is a challenge virtually all spiritual leaders deal with; that is why the Bible gives us some real insights into the causes and cures for discouragement. We have Elijah's experience in his "cave of despondency." In Exodus 15:22–27 Moses deals with it leading the Hebrews out of slavery toward the Promised Land.

The Bible makes it clear disappointment and discouragement are common experiences in life. Events sometimes disappoint us. You plan in anticipation to go see something; you work for it, you buy the ticket, but when you get there it's a dud, and you're disappointed. Things tend to disappoint us. We buy things we want and then we get them, and they disappoint us. The greatest source of discouragement is usually people. People who put us down, who do not appreciate what we do for them, who break their promises.

Lionhearted pastors understand that to make it in ministry you have to learn to deal with people. If anybody was a pro at dealing with discouraging people, it was Moses. He had to have been the most patient man around in his day. No man has ever put up with more complaining.

> Then Moses led Israel from the Red Sea and they went into the desert of Shur. For three days they traveled into the desert without finding water. When they came to Marah, they could not drink its water because it was bitter, that is why the place is called Marah." (Exodus 15:22–23 NIV)

Beyond every mountain, there is always a valley.

Israel had just experienced a great victory at the Red Sea. They were flying high. It must have been an exhilarating experience to see the Egyptian army defeated so dramatically. In the first part of Exodus 15, they are singing a song of praise, "God has delivered us. What a great day! We are unbeatable! We're invincible!" Three days later, they are grumbling and murmuring. Each new day brings its own problems.

God uses disappointment to test our trust in Him.

> So Moses cried out to the LORD for help, and the LORD showed him a piece of wood. Moses threw it into the water, and this made the water good to drink. It was there at Marah that the LORD set before them the following decree as a standard to test their faithfulness to him. (Exodus 15:25 NLT)

God led them to Marah, a bitter disappointment, to test their reaction: "Do they really trust Me?" God was not testing them at the Red Sea. He just opened the waters based on Moses's faith. I believe God's character was revealed at the Red Sea, and man's character was revealed at Marah. Lionhearted pastors/leaders know our character is revealed in the daily irritations, in the frustrations of ministry.

One of the most common causes of discouragement is being criticized and attacked by people in the church. It reminds me of what the Hebrews did with Moses: "So the people grumbled against Moses saying, 'What are we to drink?'" (Exodus 15:24 NIV). This a typical response for people. They complain, gripe, grumble and criticize their leader.

Many times, pastors feel like they work hard, love people, serve with intensity, and nothing happens. I went through a time of deep discouragement in one of the churches I served. Looking back on it, it was because I was working as hard as I could, connecting with people though every possible means at my disposal, but the church was just dead in the water.

Give your disappointments to God.

A lionhearted pastor will do what Moses did: "Then Moses cried out to the Lord" (Exodus 15:25 NIV). You give it to God and let Him have it! When you are disappointed, don't talk to others about it but talk to the Lord. "Cast all your cares on Him, because He cares for you" (1 Peter 5:7 NIV).

Instead of holding a pity party, focus on the good that God can bring you out of this discouraging time. "Then Moses cried unto the Lord and the Lord showed him a piece of wood and he threw it into the water and the water became sweet" (Exodus 15:25 NIV). God can bring good even out of things people do to us maliciously. God can provide a miraculous solution.

Lionhearted pastors are persistent in their faith. They understand it is easy to miss God's great blessing when they give up too soon. Exodus 15:27 (NIV) says: "Then they came to Elim where there were twelve springs and seventy palm trees, and they camped near the water." Frequently the places of delight and disappointment are only a short distance from each other. Elim and Marah are five miles apart.

My observation is that too often we stop too soon. We stop at Marah and get discouraged, and it's distasteful, and we stay there. Lionhearted pastors do not admit defeat; they know Elim is right around the corner.

The lionhearted leader will choose resilience over disappointment. Rely on the promises of God and choose to be encouraged rather than discouraged. God is calling you to overcome your disappointment by taking a gigantic step of faith.

I am always amazed when, after days of rain and darkness, one morning you get up and the gray and drizzle are gone, the sky is clear, and everything is beautiful again. The lionhearted leader will experience this if he or she just persists through the gray and rainy days of ministry.

Ministry Thunderstorms

The Grace Place Church is located on the east coast of South Florida, and we are familiar with all kinds of storms. During the summer months we have what we call "afternoon thunderstorms." The day may start out sunny, bright, and beautiful, but by early afternoon the skies get black, the wind starts blowing furiously, the lightning flashes, the thunder rolls, and the rain can be blinding. When you look out of a window, it looks like everything is going to blow away.

The lionhearted pastor/leader understands these storms pass over very quickly and move on. When I first started in ministry, the "ministry thunderstorms" would keep me awake at night. I would fret and stew over them and feel like the church was going to fall apart.

After over four decades in ministry, I understand now it's just another thunderstorm and generally do not fret about it, lose sleep over it, or let it distract me from what I am supposed to be doing. The combination of experience, maturity, and deeper trust in God transforms how you deal with a "ministry thunderstorm."

Within a few months of completing our phase one building project, we went through one of these thunderstorms. A negatite started a crusade to get rid of me. He went to elders, staff members, and anyone else he thought might have influence and attempted to polarize them against me.

When I found out what he was doing, I addressed the issue with the staff and then with the elders. I shared with them what Paul says about such people in Romans 16:17–18 (NIV): "I urge you, brothers, to watch out for those who cause divisions and put obstacles in your way that are contrary to the teaching you have learned. Keep away from them. For such people are not serving our Lord Christ, but their own appetites. By smooth talk and flattery, they deceive the minds of *naive* people" (emphasis mine).

Paul was instructing Christians in Rome and Christians in our town who were being negatively influenced by negatites to have nothing to do with them. By isolating them, you are reducing their opportunities to negatively influence more people.

Not long after identifying this man as a divisive person, he came to my office in tears and said, "Rick, I feel like a little boy who had a temper tantrum and beat his pillow against a pole, and the feathers have flown everywhere, and I don't know what to do about it." After talking to him for a while about what he had attempted to do and the damage it caused, I accepted his apology, and today we are friends.

I know that responding to these challenges biblically is critically important. It takes courage to be a lionhearted pastor/leader because Satan is going to use every tactic possible to wreak destruction on a pastor and a church that determine they are going to work together to advance the kingdom of Christ.

Ministry Tropical Storms

Tropical storms have names; depending on their strength, they can inflict severe damage to property, plants, trees, and more.

Several months after the ministry thunderstorm, my sons and I were on a hunting trip in Alabama when I received an urgent call from my assistant. She told me someone had gotten into our bookkeeper's computer records and downloaded our contribution data and sent fraudulent end-of-the-year financial statements to the congregation. The financial statements had a note on the bottom "from me," making it appear I was trying to figure out how much money people were earning based upon their contributions. In addition to all this, they had stolen stationery and envelopes from the church. (We later learned the importance of securing those records through passwords and a variety of other measures to make sure only two or three people had access to that information.)

My sons and I immediately returned to Florida, and the following weekend I publicly addressed the fraudulent information and explained what had happened. I then went on to explain how we handle the privacy of contributions.

The interesting thing is that what Satan meant for destruction was something God used to build a greater level of trust. Another sidebar benefit was that offerings increased, on the average by over $1,000 per week immediately following this incident.

When this happened, I realized we were dealing with a different level of maliciousness than I had ever dealt with before. We had just built a new facility, and we were in a significant transition time for the church.

As I was praying about it, I believe God put it into perspective for me. He reminded me that during the summer months in Florida, we have violent tropical storms. On these and similar occasions, I have shared with the elders and our staff that "this is just a ministry tropical storm—a little more serious than a ministry thunderstorm, but it will soon pass, the sun will shine again, and it won't be long until we have forgotten all about it."

I want to quickly point out, however, that a pastor/leader cannot be passive about these storms and must take every step possible to address the problem promptly and decisively. God has never honored passivity and procrastination.

Ministry Category 1 to 3 Hurricanes

The difference between a thunderstorm or a tropical storm and a Category 1 to 3 hurricane is the length of the storm, the intensity of the wind, and the amount of rain you receive. Another difference is that the thunderstorm pops up unexpectedly, but the hurricane builds up on the ocean and you see and know it's coming.

I came to realize when we have dealt with a lower-level ministry hurricane that it has not "come out of the blue." It had been building for some time before it happens.

In the nearly three decades I have lived in South Florida, we have had countless hurricanes come through our area. Some of the storms have done some roof damage to our house. Others have uprooted trees. Some have done light damage to our church facilities. All of them cause inconvenience because the electricity generally goes out for a few days to a week or so. It is always uncomfortable because hurricanes typically come during the hottest days of the summer and fall. I have learned to prepare early for the storms and have my generator fuel purchased in the late spring and my shutters ready to be put on my house, etc.

I could share a lot of stories about the lower category storms we have experienced in nearly three decades of ministry in South Florida. Each of them is unique and each has done its full share of damage, but I am not going to give Satan the space in this chapter to go into the details.

Ministry Category 4 and 5 Hurricanes

One year before we moved to South Florida, Hurricane Andrew leveled the Homestead area south of Miami. The damage was so severe it took many years to rebuild Homestead. A lot of residents settled with their insurance companies and moved out of state. Others resettled in different areas of Florida.

A Category 5 hurricane leaves a path of utter destruction in its path and causes enormous fear and is very unsettling.

About a decade ago we had several catastrophic events in our church that were the equivalent of a Category 5 ministry storm. Satan used them to rob us of momentum, morale, people, and finances.

Unfortunately, I had hired some staff pastors who didn't express it when I interviewed them, but subsequent behaviors revealed they wanted to be senior pastors. Much of the damage they caused was directly connected to violation of the tenth commandment, which says: "You shall not covet your neighbor's house. You shall not covet your neighbor's wife, or his male or female servant, his ox or donkey, or anything that belongs to your neighbor" (Exodus 20:17 NIV). All of them attempted to undermine me in one way or another, and when they were unsuccessful, they would resign and take anywhere from forty to three hundred people with them and start a church in the area. We had that happen enough times that it created some real challenges for us.

During that some period, I had to release three different staff members for being engaged in ongoing homosexual relationships. One of them was very repentant, and we supported his wife while he went away for a resident treatment program. The second one just disappeared without a word. The third one attempted to lie his way out of the situation even though we had screenshots of him with his picture soliciting homosexual relationships and instant messages between him and the guy who outed him before one of their sexual encounters. He then began a Facebook assault on me personally. He stole our church database and sent a lengthy email to everyone on our church list accusing me and the people involved in outing him of just about any bazaar thing he could dream up. That email had a lot of negative impact because I knew to respond in any way would just open it up for him to continue his assault. When a person has no moral values, is a liar, and resorts to any treacherous response possible, nothing is gained by a response. My response would be that I know who I am at the core and what we have done serving this community for several decades. His attacks continued for over a year and a half. Finally, I went to the sheriff in our county and described what was going on, and after warning me about how dangerous people like this guy were, he encouraged me to be on my guard. He then had his detectives investigate and meet with my attacker, and the assault on me and the church finally stopped.

A Thousand Sleepless Nights

When all of this happened, we lost around five hundred people and with it the better part of a million dollars in tithes and offerings as well. The church owed over $3.5 million on the facilities, and it was a huge struggle to make ends meet. I didn't have a lot of people to talk to about all this to help guide me through one of the toughest times in my life and ministry journey. Many months my wife and I would front loans from our own money to the church to keep our commitments to the bank and pay our staff. We went through one period where I didn't cash a salary check for over three months to make sure staff and other bills were paid. I realized then in ways I never experienced before what being a lionhearted pastor/leader is really like.

The above events began what I call a five-year period of waking up at least one thousand nights, generally around 1:00 to 3:00 a.m. and going to the den in our house, kneeling by my favorite chair and praying until I had no more words to say. I would then sit down in that chair and ask God to speak to my spirit with whatever I needed to hear Him say. Sometimes He would bring a scripture to my mind. Other times He would bring the words of a song I had heard or something I had read to my mind. On a few occasions the Holy Spirit would speak to me, not audibly but in my spirit and give me a peace that only comes from God during those times. On a few occasions I was aware God was giving me direction.

More than anything during this time I wanted to make sure I did not react in an unforgiving or retaliatory way toward those who had done these things. God used those thousand nights of prayer to search my heart and expose to me things in my life He wanted to transform. I would never want to relive that time again, but what I learned and what God did in my heart was worth all the pain and the struggles.

In the middle of one of the Category 5 storms we went through, God gave me Joel 2:25 (International Standard Version) as one of his promises: "Then I will restore to you the years that the locust swarm devoured." That is the kind of God we serve.

CHAPTER 14

If I Had Known Then ...

If only I had known forty years ago what I know today, I would have saved myself a lot of heartache and grief. But I guess we all would prefer to live in hindsight, and perhaps we wouldn't gain the wisdom we do any other way than by trial and tribulation. Still, if I could go back to my younger self ...

I wish I had known the signs of disloyalty.

I went to a conference with C. Peter Wagner many years ago, while still a solo pastor. He said, "Some of you are going to be blessed by God in special ways, and you will start developing a multistaff ministry. When you do you will discover that the greatest gift any staff member ever gives you is loyalty." It didn't take too long after we moved from solo ministry to multistaff ministry for me to discover C. Peter Wagner was correct.

I don't think most disloyal people wake up one morning and suddenly finds themselves disloyal. Disloyalty goes through various stages before it fully reveals itself. If this attitude is checked at these early stages, it may never become a problem. *Disloyalty* sounds like a terrible word, but it progresses through some not-so-terrible-sounding stages:

• **Silo ministries**

Occasionally, I will remind our staff of the danger of "silo" ministries. Any time I have had a staff member who sees "their" ministry isolated from the other ministries and from the weekend services, it is evidence of an independent spirit. We regularly communicate with our staff that everything we do in the various ministries is really "all about the weekend!" If there is no one in the church on the weekend from a ministry, it is always because we have the wrong person in leadership.

Often in religious circles there is a maneuvering for recognition. An independent spirit caused this. An independent spirit is caused by a lack of submission to the will of those in oversight. The New Testament is full of examples of submission.

> But you know that Timothy has proved himself, because as a son with his father he has served with me in the work of the gospel. (Philippians 2:22 NIV)

> Suppose one of you has a servant plowing or looking after the sheep. Will he say to the servant when he comes in from the field, "Come along now and sit down to eat"? Won't he rather say, "Prepare my supper, get yourself ready and wait on me while I eat and drink; after that you may eat and drink"? Will he thank the servant because he did what he was told to do? So, you also, when you have done everything you were told to do, should say, "We are unworthy servants; we have only done our duty." (Luke 17:7–10 NIV)

- **Craving the spotlight**

If our relationship with God is weak, we can easily shift our desires from receiving the approval of God to that of others. We begin promoting ourselves in order that we might receive personal recognition rather than ministering to people as the Lord directs us. Though we may think we love people, we don't. We love the praise of people.

When a staff member has the wrong motivations, he will start collecting a group of admirers that form a clique, and they isolate themselves from others in the church. In this way he gathers disciples to him who will help him feed his ego and his thirst for recognition. Soon he begins to stir up discontent that becomes a challenge to spiritual leadership.

> Whoever heeds discipline shows the way to life, but whoever ignores correction leads others astray. (Proverbs 10:17 NIV)

> Who is wise and understanding among you? Let them show it by their good life, by deeds done in the humility that comes from wisdom. But if you harbor bitter envy and selfish ambition in your hearts, do not boast about it or deny the truth. Such "wisdom" does not come down from heaven but is earthly, unspiritual, demonic. For where you have envy and selfish ambition, there you find disorder and every evil practice. (James 3:13– 16 NIV)

When the staff member resigns or is let go, they take their little group with them and then start their own church.

If a leader has a strong personal ambition, he will have little love for the flock of God. He will not have a servant's heart, and a leader must be first and foremost a servant.

> Am I now trying to win the approval of human beings, or of God? Or am I trying to please people? If I were still trying to please people, I would not be a servant of Christ. (Galatians 1:10 NIV)

> Be careful not to practice your righteousness in front of others to be seen by them. If you do, you will have no reward from your Father in heaven. (Matthew 6:1 NIV)

• **Arrogance and Pride**

When a man begins to think too highly of himself and his own ministry, he begins to develop an attitude of spiritual pride. As a result, he tries to impress others with his wonderful ideas. He then is unwilling to listen to your suggestions, input, and/or correction. I have had young developing leaders who cannot see with the same eyes of experience that a more mature leader can. Unfortunately, they do not have all the information the pastor has and usually do not have a clear understanding as to how a particular decision by leadership fits within the totality of the overall vision of the church.

Solomon had some incredible words of wisdom about the devastating effect pride has on a person and why it can do so much damage to the church:

> Do you see a person wise in their own eyes? There is more hope for a fool than for them. (Proverbs 26:12 NIV)

The way of fools seems right to them, but the wise listen to advice. (Proverbs 12:15 NIV)

Listen to advice and accept discipline, and at the end you will be counted among the wise. (Proverbs 19:20 NIV)

- **Passive/aggressive response**

My dad used to tell the story of the little boy who was given a timeout and had to sit in a chair for a certain period. When asked what he was doing, he said, "I am sitting down on the outside, but standing up on the inside."

I see this behavior in people who say yes, but then their actions say no. They will tell you what you want to hear but turn around and do it their way anyway. Many times, I will see this behavior with an attitude of detachment in meetings or activities we do with the staff. This behavior will always lead to destructive disloyalty.

- **Criticism**

As a person's disloyalty progresses, it inevitably leads to a critical attitude toward the pastor among the parishioners. Many times, it hinders the way the church functions. If the leadership rejects a pastor's ideas, he may feel there must be something wrong with their judgment and discernment. His spiritual pride is at stake. He begins to use his own ideas as a criterion for the judgment of all the decisions of the overseers. As a result, he develops a critical spirit toward the church's leadership. "Deceit is in the hearts of those who plot evil, but those who promote peace have joy" (Proverbs 12:20 NIV).

The disloyal person then gossips against the leadership in progressive degrees of severity. He begins by speaking against those faults and frailties in the leadership that are obvious to all, and not necessarily related to spiritual qualifications. He then moves to more obscure areas. Those around him believe him because he was "right" about other things.

We have seen how disloyalty develops and ultimately manifests itself in separation and ruin. Disloyalty is not always easy to see externally, and that is why many times it goes unchecked in the early stages. If disloyalty is not recognized and dealt with, it will ultimately bring division to the work of God. It is important that we as individuals use these tests on ourselves.

We should allow the Holy Spirit to examine our hearts in the pure light of God's Word. If we catch ourselves in the early stages, we must confess, repent, and reconcile. We should also seek accountability for our heart problems with those God has placed in authority over us. As we work and live together with the people of God, let us endeavor "to keep the unity of the Spirit in the bond of peace" (Ephesians 4:3 NIV).

I wish I had known some staff members are liars and thieves.

I grew up in a family that placed a high value on honesty of every kind. Telling a lie was a guaranteed trip to what I would call the "woodshed," which happened to be my bedroom, where the "board of wisdom and knowledge" was applied to the "seat of understanding." I knew my dad meant business and do not remember ever lying to him to avoid the consequences.

As a result, lying and/or stealing has never been a significant issue with me. To this day, if I do something where I have shared something that could cause someone to come to the wrong conclusion, my conscience will not allow me to sleep and move on until I have clarified things.

The ninth commandment says, "You shall not give false testimony against your neighbor" (Exodus 20:16 NIV). All through the Bible, God emphasizes repeatedly the importance of telling the truth—all the time and in all situations. Growing up and as an adult, I don't remember ever stealing something from anyone either. I handle a lot of church funds and have an unlimited expense account. It would never occur to me to use those funds personally.

I have had staff members use church funds to pay for their spouse's birthday party, buy things for themselves, or even buy gifts for others. (When the bookkeeper catches it, we make them repay it, and by the time we are through dealing with it—and we put them on a very short leash—most of them will resign.) Most of these staff members seemingly have no concern about lying, cheating, or stealing; it is just a way of life for them.

Some years ago, we had a couple of staff members who were not returning the tithe to the church. When I talked to them individually, they both told me they had opened new checking accounts and their tithes must not have been paid automatically from their accounts. I let them know that this was hard to believe, and it also told me more than I wanted to know about how they managed their finances. Unfortunately, those two guys were just the tip of the iceberg of staff I have had who were confirmed, habitual, and dangerous liars.

I wish I had known to watch the spouses of staff members better.

You can figure out a lot about what is really going on with staff members by watching their wives. When a wife becomes detached from the church—for example, she quits volunteering for a ministry in which she's been involved or participating in staff events or activities, or the couple starts moving from the middle pews into the back row, it generally means they are separating themselves, and the husband is considering leaving.

I also watch for what their attitude is like toward myself or my wife; when it has taken a nosedive or is distant, it is obvious something negative is going on. Many times, the guys can cover it up, but the wives will give it away virtually every time.

I wish I had known the difference between a hireling and a shepherd.

The hired hand is not the shepherd who owns the sheep. So, when he sees the wolf coming, he abandons the sheep and runs away. Then the wolf attacks the flock and scatters it. The man runs away because he is a hired hand and cares nothing for the sheep. (John 10:12–13 NIV)

To recap, the shepherd sees what they are doing as a ministry; the hireling sees it as a job. When I hear a staff member referring to what they are doing as "my job," I will make a mental note of it, and when I meet with them one-on-one, I will always remind them we don't give people jobs; we only give them the opportunity to serve and minister to those with whom they are assigned to work.

Likewise, when a staff member starts referring to me as a "boss," it is an indicator they are seeing their ministry assignment as a job. Almost without fail I have reminded them that people with jobs have bosses, but people with ministries have pastors who lead them.

A hireling will quit with no concern about how their departure affects the ministry they were leading. In fact, I have had plenty of hirelings who tried to destroy the ministry they were leading when they left the church.

Prior to coming to Stuart to pastor The Grace Place, I resigned from four different churches during the years leading up to coming to this church. I always felt when people said I left those churches in better shape than I found them, it was a compliment to the church. I would never have wanted the church to fall apart because I left. Because of the ethics I had in my earlier days of hiring staff, it never really dawned on me there would be people I would hire who would attempt to destroy the ministry they were leading when they left.

I wish I had known to look for people who undersell and overperform.

We must be careful to validate the claims some people make on their resumes that sound like they are almost too good to be true. I am always amazed when people include their interview numbers, programs, etc. that are so good you cannot imagine why they didn't stay where they were.

It has always been a part of my personality to undersell my abilities and accomplishments. I would much rather have people be surprised by what we accomplish rather than disappointed because of what we couldn't or didn't do.

Developing a good work ethic is essential if we are going to accomplish things that bring value to our ministries. A good work ethic means being a self-starter, someone who knows how to get up and get started every day without having to be prodded, coaxed, or threatened. Just be aware if you are not adding value, you are a liability.

Many people in ministry would take a gigantic step forward if they just learned to work. My dad died when I was fourteen years old, and I began working every day after school. By the time I was sixteen, I was subcontracting drywall labor and had my own crew working for me. Somewhere along the way I came to a clear understanding that if I wasn't producing, I wasn't doing what I was supposed to do. When you are subcontracting, you figure out real fast that if the hammers and saws are resting, you are not only not making money, but you are also losing money in a hurry.

Pastors are notorious for being lazy. Most of the guys I have hired who came from small churches have a huge problem dealing with our structured culture for staff members. Lots of them love to drag in around 10:00 or 11:00 a.m., do a few things, and then leave around 2:00 or 3:00 p.m. and feel like they have put in a full day.

One of those guys worked for me for a brief period. I was talking to him about his short workdays and not getting things done, and he had the audacity to tell me he was working eighty hours a week. I handed him a piece of paper and said, "tell me how many hours you have worked so far this week."

His "work" included eating breakfast and dinner with his family (because they were a part of his ministry). It included his time at the gym, grocery shopping, and anything else in his personal world. I would love to see what would happen if he told a secular employer he was working eighty hours a week with all that stuff included. Lionhearted pastors are not afraid of work.

I wish I had known to avoid people who blow up their ministry bridges.

I have observed that people who blow up their ministry bridges will do everything they can to keep you from contacting their former senior pastor or supervisor from previous ministries. They are also very quick to criticize their former leaders and cannot seem to see anything they have done wrong. If you want to avoid a lot of trouble, just stay away from more than an introductory meeting with them.

When I am interviewing potential staff members, I remind them if they are going to be successful in doing what we are asking them to do, they must "start well, run well, and end well."

I have lived and served in ministry long enough to see people who are regularly blowing up their ministry bridges get stuck at a tiny ministry island they cannot escape. People who do not blow up their ministry bridges will frequently discover the bridge they walked over will lead them to another ministry opportunity that is better than anything they could imagine. That is why it is so important to never leave a ministry because you are angry or reacting to something that happens.

I wish I had known to hire slower and fire faster.

I am not a naturally patient person. We put together goals and strategies and plans for set periods, and many times we need to hire a leader for an area of ministry development that is a part of those plans. At times I have hired the wrong people and knew it within a matter of weeks or a couple of months. Instead of finding a way to end their tenure in a God-honoring way, I have opted to attempt to coach them into fitting their assignment. Most of the time that has been the equivalent to trying to make a prince out of a frog. People either have it or they don't, and there is every little you can do to help people become something they are not.

Generally, that happens when I hire too fast and then fail to end the relationship earlier rather than later. I know from my interactions with other pastors I am not the only one who struggles with these issues.

It is a good thing God is in the restoration business, even when we make bad decisions.

CHAPTER 15

The Rewards of Lionhearted Leadership

God has used A. W. Tozer's words to give me hope in what has seemed at times to be hopeless circumstances. He said, "It is doubtful whether God can bless a man greatly until he has hurt him deeply." It is my observation God uses the storms of conflict in relationships to accomplish His deeper work in our character. I cannot love my enemies in my own strength. That takes graduate-level grace. God brings us through these testing times as preparation for greater use in the kingdom. We must pass the grace test first.

I have no idea how many pastors with whom I have met who are going through times of great difficulty. Sometimes it is because of poor financial decisions, others because they have been betrayed by a former staff member who has stolen one third to half of their congregation, others because of a legal challenge.

When they come to me for insight and counsel, most of the time I encourage them to stay with the church and see it through this storm and tell them the ministry sun will shine again. It seems to me most of them cannot see their way through what they are dealing with, and they leave. Sometimes they go to another church, and in a matter of a few years they are going through another storm. I have said to myself so many times that they would have been so much better off to have stayed where they were and work through whatever was going on than to have bolted and run.

Leadership is always hard, and there are going to be some serious bumps along our ministry roads. I have said many times: "You never know the skill of a boat captain until you see him guide his ship through the worst of storms." Anyone with modest skills can pilot the boat though calm waters; it is the storm that separates the men from the boys.

After leading The Grace Place through some pretty major storms, there are some things I have learned that might help you to continue to lead even though you may be going through one of those tough leadership places.

You Are Always Teaching by Example

Lionhearted leaders always remember the people they are leading are always watching them. In fact, most of us teach more by what people see than what we say. Great messages that are not backed up by a consistent example are totally ineffective. As my dad used to tell me, "Who you are speaks so loudly no one can hear what you say." The tough place in the leadership journey gives us the opportunity to teach by example.

Those you lead will see real commitment to the kingdom. Commitment is always seen through resilience and perseverance.

My wife and I have been married for many decades. Long-term marriages are built on the foundation of deep commitment to each other and to the marriage. It is relatively easy to find passages of scripture on commitment and preach sermons about how important it is, but until it is fleshed out in our lives, it is not convincing.

When the people you lead see commitment to their church and to the kingdom of God, they can truly understand what it looks like. If they see me ready to quit when I encounter a difficult place, they will tend to do the same thing with their work and their marriages.

A lionhearted leader gets their courage from *trusting in God's promises*. There are hundreds of promises in the Bible that apply to the circumstances we are facing. Over the years God has given me some promises that were directly connected to what we were dealing with at the time.

We lost around two hundred people over a two-week period because we had to release one of our pastors for active homosexuality. He stole the church's database and sent out an email full of lies. I refused to respond to it because when someone has no moral values, he can lie with no compunction of conscience. God gave me Joel 2:25 NIV as my promise in dealing with this. God says in that verse "he will restore what the locust has eaten." I have kept that promise now for many years. It has given me the courage to move forward and not be bogged down with fear.

Several years ago, after losing around three hundred people to another staff member who was "starting" a church in our area, our offerings dropped off significantly, and we still had $3.5 million of debt. I was praying about the debt and felt like God shared with me He did not want us to be a "slave to debt," and he was going to set us free. After several years of praying a circle around that principle, in one day God set us free.

Had I left during those challenging times, we would have never seen these promises fulfilled. I would have missed some of the greatest blessings of my ministry journey, and the church would probably never have experienced seeing firsthand what God can do. God does not promise us an easy road; He does promise to be there and do what He says He will do.

The tough places in ministry enable the lionhearted leader to *model godly character*. God will use those places to purify our motives, produce humility, and see our character defects like no other experiences in life or ministry. I have spent many nights in prayer as we have gone through some of these difficult places in ministry. God has been able to show me myself in ways I would have never seen in the pleasant places. One of my prayers over the years when we were dealing with those negative experiences was, "show me myself and help my see any wicked ways in me."

"Only God" Experiences

I have personally seen the following come true as a direct result of my faith and ministry.

"Only God" can sustain you through the darkest nights.

"Only God" can transform the negative experiences into positives.

"Only God" can do the miraculous.

A Deeper Level of Trust and Comradery with Church Leaders

I have also experienced the following:

- Tough times separate the wheat from the chaff.
- You know who can and cannot be trusted.
- You wept and laughed together.
- The lay leadership knows the leader can be counted on to "stick with it" in the future.

Personal Rewards

There is a deep satisfaction in knowing you have not run away from a problem but found a way to work through it and maintain self-respect. Staying with the church during the tough times has a way of creating generosity and creating sensitivity toward other leaders who are going through challenging times.

I remember many times being present at the "end of life" of someone who has lived his or her life well. You can always see it in the lives of their closest friends and family. There is still grief, but the hope that is present during that time is profound. I have also been there for people who lived selfish lives. I have seen families in turmoil over the lives of people who were fun to be around and even well-liked but were unwise in their investments in others.

There is a huge benefit to being able to lay your head on the pillow at night and know that you did everything within your calling and gift set for the kingdom. Lionhearted leaders live with this goal in mind. It drives them to complete their God-given tasks, motivate people, and keep others focused on the real goal, which is to build the kingdom of Heaven.

These leaders know that they are the most fulfilled when they are accomplishing these goals. Each lionhearted leader also realizes that it's all about pointing people to Jesus and making His name famous. It really is all about Him. It's not about money or prestige. The goal is to see Jesus work through the lives of everyday people and help them to see their purpose in the kingdom as well.

What Is at Stake?

The fear for most of us is that we are missing a great opportunity in another place—that if we stay, we will have to "go down with the ship." While there may be instances where leaving is the right thing to do, many times it spells disaster for the organization, and the fallout is disillusioned parishioners. People follow people, and when a pastor exits, especially during tough times, there are many who will not continue the journey with the organization they left behind.

So, if you do leave, make sure that it is God's calling and not your desire to mend a broken ego or escape a potentially bad situation. As Christian leaders, we are to pilot the ship toward God's calling. Though God will work despite our fallacies, we must understand that there is always a cost for running.

As a kid, I always loved the story of Jonah and the whale. Jonah, as you recall, runs from God's calling to bring about repentance of the Ninevites. To stay safe, he decides to go in the opposite direction. God sends a big fish to carry Jonah back, and he decides that God's way is better and finally approaches the king of Nineveh.

After the Ninevites repent, Jonah has a bad attitude. He is emotionally spent, and the Bible never says anything more about Jonah. I know this is probably not hermeneutically sound, but I believe that one reason you don't hear about Jonah anymore is that he was unwilling to do the difficult work that God called him to do, and his attitude was such that God could not use him anymore. He had the talent, the call of God, and the reputation with the people to make a difference. What he didn't have was the ability to let go of the past, and he lost his passion for the things of God. God did not abandon Jonah; he abandoned his call.

When times get tough, it's easy to abandon our call. It's easy to take the easy way out. If you hang in there, you can see God do an incredible work. When you do, make sure you recognize it and don't look through your own lens just to see how it affects you, but how it has helped build the church and God's kingdom.

Pastoral leadership is all about gaining ground and influencing people for the kingdom. I know God has great plans for you, and it's my prayer that you will take these words and put them into practice. If you do, then you will be free to be a lionhearted leader.

One day I hope I hear Jesus say, "Well done, my good and faithful servant."

CHAPTER 16

Lionhearted Forgiveness—Eric Addison wrote this last chapter with his father's consent four weeks before his passing.

Forgiveness allows us to have no unfinished business before we leave this life. What King Richard knew was that his legacy would be the only thing that would survive after he was gone.

Christlike forgiveness can set us free to be who God called us to be. When we come to the end of our lives, do we want to hear, "You let resentments and issues with forgiveness keep you from my best for your life" or "Well done, my good and faithful servant?" Keep in mind that lionhearted leaders have the courage to move forward no matter the size of the opposing force.

For many of us, holding onto resentments and failing to forgive will be the arrows that will bring us down. If you want to be a long-haul or lionhearted leader, then you need to have a reputation for forgiveness. You must take away Satan's ability to steal your focus from Christ and His calling on your life.

A lionhearted leader will be able to show their church what *true forgiveness* looks like. When you go through some of the vicious attacks all lionhearted leaders will inevitably face, there are ample opportunities to practice forgiveness. When we flesh it out, our response does more to teach our congregation and the leaders in our churches about true forgiveness than a sermon we stand on a stage to deliver.

Richard first understood true forgiveness from his mother, who was widowed at the age of thirty-six when a drunk driver killed his dad. His parents had very little money when he died. They lived in a house owned by the church, and he had a few thousand dollars of life insurance. His mom was left with five children to raise on her own—Richard being the oldest at fourteen years old, with his youngest sibling just two.

A lot of people encouraged his mom to find someone to sue over his dad's accident. His mom kept saying, "Suing is not going to bring my husband back; it will make us continue to relive his death and will make me and my children angry and vengeful."

Over the remaining thirty-nine years of his mom's life, she was never angry (maybe sometimes a little confused) over his dad's death. Her refusal to be vengeful had an amazing impact on the family. life. None of the siblings have ever struggled with anger toward the man responsible for their dad's death; in fact, they never knew his name. They felt that knowing more about him would not bring their dad back and would not change anything for the better in their lives.

Many pastors have allowed their tough ministry experiences to cause them to throw in the white towel of surrender and leave vocational ministry. Frequently, they are embittered and negative about the church and cynical about Christians in general.

Forgiveness allows us to move forward and not be tethered to the past. It allows us to experience the best of God's future blessings.

Because ministry is made of relationships, forgiveness must be a foundation upon which life change can happen. *Forgiveness* is a misunderstood and often misused word. It describes the ability to not hold on to feelings of hurt or resentment toward a person who has wronged you.

The idea of "forgive and forget" is deceiving though because in many cases forgetting would not be wise.

There are pastors who have been hurt by parishioners, other pastors, and even spouses, and it destroys their ability to minister. In fact, one could say that forgiveness is at the heart of any long-term ministry. While the word *forgiveness* is easy to say, the practice of it is difficult to do.

Let's unpack what forgiveness is *not:*

1. Forgiveness is not giving someone a license to hurt us over and over. Abuse is never a good thing. Allowing people to abuse us is not forgiveness. Jesus did not say," Give your enemies the ability to hurt you again." He said, "Do good to those who persecute you."

2. Forgiveness is not a public display of affection for your enemy. Forgiveness is a heart issue. It affects your thought patterns. It keeps your focus on what's important. Resentment steels your focus and turns it into a kind of cancer. Many people publicly display how they have forgiven someone for the rest of us to find out it was all only a show. Satan loves to display hypocrisy in all its forms, and people know if you are being sincere. I cannot tell you how many staff members and pastors will quit a ministry calling because they cannot overcome a hurt in their lives.

3. Forgiveness is not an instant event. In our technology-based culture, we want everything to be instant. We want pain to heal overnight. We want people to get over their perceived pain

toward us as well. As pastors and ministry leaders, we have a tough time believing that we can cause anyone else pain. Forgiveness is a process, and it is intentional. We should look at our own motives and actions through rose-colored glasses while seeing the actions of everyone else in a much darker light. It is important to have people that we are accountable to to show us the areas where we are wrong.

4. Forgiveness does not depend on the offender. The offended is solely responsible to forgive. Don't wait for others to come around to release the pain they caused you. Some people will never see what they have done. If you do this, you are allowing them to hurt you repeatedly.

So how do we show true forgiveness? First, we need to acknowledge the hurt. Ignoring the fact that someone has wronged us only delays the healing. Truth is especially important when it comes to bringing issues to light. A surgeon can't operate in the dark. Neither can we begin the healing process if there are unconfessed resentments. Sometimes this involves a critical conversation with those who have hurt us. If the person is receptive to us, and the slight was a mere mistake, then a conversation is needed.

However, the worst wounds are the ones from people who have malicious intent. Maybe the person who wrongs you is the product of jealousy or blind ambition. Maybe they are hurt and are projecting their pain onto you. Whatever the case, beware of the people who will never come around and admit they are wrong. In these cases, forgiveness is just for you. You don't hold anything against them. But you are not inviting them into your inner circle either. When you can see them in public, and it doesn't affect your attitude, then you know you are successful at forgiving.

There is a reality that is sometimes difficult to admit in life. Many people are not meant to go on the journey with you. You have a calling. God chose you to pastor your area of ministry. You are unique and gifted for that ministry. Your focus must be moving the ball forward to further the kingdom. Unconfessed resentments lead to strife and eventually division, so you just can't afford to hold onto them.

Second, we need to release the offending person to God. It helps to remember that God loves that person as much as He loves you. If God is our heavenly Father, do you think He plays favorites?

While He cares about what was done to you, He also cares about the other's success and working His purposes in those with whom we disagree. When God says, "Revenge is mine, I will repay," He is taking the authority away from us humans and placing it in His own hands. God can see things that we cannot see. We think we know others' motives, but God can see directly into the heart. He knows what led to that action. He knows the best way to achieve restoration of your heart … and that of another.

Apostle Paul wrote: "Dear Friends, never take revenge. Leave room for God's wrath. For the Scriptures say, 'Vengeance is Mine, I will repay, says the Lord.'" (Deuteronomy, Chapter/Verse NLT) When he says leave room for God's wrath, it simply means let God choose how He admonishes a sinner.

If you find yourself talking negatively about people who have hurt you, then resentment has made an impact on your attitude. From there it finds its way to your heart without much of a filter and is corroding like a cancer. Forgiveness is not trust. You don't have to let others hurt you repeatedly. But you do need to forgive for yourself and for God. And the only way to truly master forgiveness is to give up control and rely on the power of the Holy Spirit.

EPILOGUE

(by Karon Addison, Wife)

Rick and I met in the summer of 1973 after we had both graduated from high school. Rick was traveling with a Bible college quartet. I was planning to attend the Bible college in South Florida in the fall, near where he and his family lived.

That summer we met at church and talked. He wrote me a couple letters while on tour that summer, and I was flattered. He later said to me he had told his mother he'd met the girl he was going to marry. I enrolled in the Bible college to get my teaching degree, and he enrolled in the ministry program. We begin dating that fall, and several dates later, Rick asked me a serious question: "If things progressed with our relationship would you be against being a pastor's wife?" He shared that he had a call to ministry and did not want to proceed dating me if it was something I would not consider.

I thought and prayed about that question for a week, and then at the ripe age of eighteen said I would be OK with it. Looking back at this time, I am so thankful for the maturity Rick had in choosing a mate … my criteria at the time was tough-looking guys and sharp cars!

Things progressed in our relationship to the point of "going steady" by Christmas. After the holidays, Rick popped the question to me about marriage. I said yes, of course! We settled on the date, August 23, 1974.

So, this country girl of nineteen began life with this "one of a kind" man, serving alongside him for almost forty-eight exciting years.

In all the five churches we have pastored over the forty-three years we've been in ministry, I have never doubted Rick's integrity, his call to ministry, and his love for God. He always lived life on purpose. He never gave me pause to question him over the years. I remember so vividly his sincere desire to be a pastor and make a difference for the kingdom. He began setting goals and then implementing those at each church we pastored.

In our first three churches God helped us mature as we worked to bring healing to each after the former leadership had caused a division. Even at this early age, we allowed God to use the difficult circumstances we encountered to grow us closer together and in our own personal spiritual walk.

When I would mention discouragement or hurt over a situation, he would say "Karon, I refuse to give up on people!" and he demonstrated that over and over.

With my practical, simple faith in a God bigger than anything we were facing, I would put the motto "bloom where you are planted" into action alongside Rick. I allowed God to open my heart to see areas of opportunity and worked alongside my husband to make a difference for the kingdom. That put me into some awkward places when we needed a pianist, and all I could do was type!

Not all pastors' wives have the privilege (much less the desire) to work alongside their husbands in ministry. I believe our lives were unique from the beginning because of Rick's heart for ministry and my acceptance of that. I never felt like I was playing second fiddle—I understood his sincere desire to do and be all God wanted him to be. I felt very strongly that I would answer to God if I distracted him from his call or stood in his way as it says in Psalm 105:15 (NIV): "Touch not mine anointed ones, and do my prophets no harm." This did not make him perfect, nor did it make me a wimp, but it did add a dimension to our lives in which we carefully looked at the responsibility entrusted to us.

As time has passed, and I interact with other people in leadership, I see more than ever there must be a genuineness and sincerity in what you are called to do. I have seen people begin in ministry with a splash and end with a plop. I have always said that "it is the person who is a plodder who will make it in ministry, not just a flash in the pan."

Looking back on these forty-three years of ministry, it seems like it's all gone by in just a blink of an eye. Each place we went we lived to the fullest. God has blessed our efforts, and lives have been changed. With God's help, each church we left was better off than before. There have been hundreds of couples Rick counseled for marriage, children he dedicated to God, believers who were baptized—all brought pure joy to this pastor who lived for an audience of One!

Living with this lionhearted man has been an absolute challenge in a good way. I have grown in my love of Christ and in living with purpose in a world that needs a steadfast leader. I have been stretched and pulled to be a be a leader in my own right alongside a man who lived life with purpose … on steroids.

Printed in the United States
by Baker & Taylor Publisher Services